Anxiety Disorders Interview Schedule for DSM-IV

Lifetime Version

Client Interview Schedule

Peter A. DiNardo
Timothy A. Brown
David H. Barlow

OXFORD
UNIVERSITY PRESS

OXFORD
UNIVERSITY PRESS

Oxford University Press, Inc., publishes works that further
Oxford University's objective of excellence
in research, scholarship, and education.

Oxford New York
Auckland Cape Town Dar es Salaam Hong Kong Karachi
Kuala Lumpur Madrid Melbourne Mexico City Nairobi
New Delhi Shanghai Taipei Toronto

With offices in
Argentina Austria Brazil Chile Czech Republic France Greece
Guatemala Hungary Italy Japan Poland Portugal Singapore
South Korea Switzerland Thailand Turkey Ukraine Vietnam

Published by Oxford University Press, Inc.
198 Madison Avenue, New York, New York 10016

www.oup.com

Oxford is a registered trademark of Oxford University Press

ISBN 978-0-19-518389-4

9 8 7 6

Printed in the United States of America
on acid-free paper

ABOUT THE AUTHORS

Peter A. DiNardo received his PhD in Clinical Psychology from Washington University in 1974. He is presently professor of psychology at the State University of New York, College at Oneonta, and he has been a consultant to the Phobia and Anxiety Disorders Clinic at the Center for Stress and Anxiety Disorders since 1982. His current research interests include diagnostic reliability of DSM–IV anxiety disorders and etiological factors in specific phobias.

Timothy A. Brown received his PsyD from the Virginia Consortium for Professional Psychology in 1988. He has published numerous scientific articles and chapters in the area of anxiety disorders. Presently, he is associate director of the Center for Anxiety and Related Disorders at Boston University and research associate/professor in the psychology department at Boston University. He has been a consultant to the National Institute of Mental Health on the evaluation of psychosocial and pharmacological treatments for anxiety disorders, and he has served as a consultant for large-scale projects focusing on the assessment and diagnosis of anxiety disorders using DSM–IV criteria. In addition, he was a member of the DSM–IV Anxiety Disorders Sub-Workgroup for generalized anxiety disorders and mixed anxiety depression. Recently, his research has focused on the classification of anxiety disorders, the development and evaluation of short- and long-term outcome of psychosocial treatments for anxiety disorders, and the nature and assessment of panic and generalized anxiety disorder.

David H. Barlow received his PhD from the University of Vermont in 1969, and he has published 15 books and more than 200 articles and chapters, mostly in the areas of anxiety disorders, sexual problems, and clinical research methodology. His recent books include *Clinical Handbook of Psychological Disorders: A Step-by-Step Treatment Manual—Second Edition* (1993), *Anxiety and Its Disorders: The Nature and Treatment of Anxiety and Panic* (1988), and *Mastery of Your Anxiety and Panic—Second Edition and Agoraphobia Supplement Therapist Guide,* coauthored by Michelle Craske (1994). Dr. Barlow was formerly professor of psychiatry and psychology at Brown University and Distinguished Professor in the Department of Psychology at the University at Albany–State University of New York. Currently, he is professor of psychology, director of the Clinical Training Program, and director of the Center for Anxiety and Related Disorders at Boston University. Dr. Barlow is also past president of the Division of Clinical Psychology of the American Psychological Association. He has been a consultant to the National Institute of Mental Health (NIMH) and the National Institutes of Health since 1973 and was recently awarded a merit award from the NIMH for "research competence and productivity that are distinctly superior." He was a member of the DSM–IV Task Force. The major objective of his work for the last 15 years has been the development of new treatments for anxiety disorders.

Name: ______________________

Date of Interview: ______________________

Address: ______________________

____

Interviewer: ______________________

Family Income: ______________________

Phone (home): ______________________

(work): ______________________

Number of Dependents: ______________________

Fee for Interview: ______________________

Date of Birth: ______________________

Insurance Plan: ______________________

Race: ______________________

ADIS Number: ______________________

Sex: ___ M ___ F

Marital Status:

___ Married	____________	Date
___ Single	____________	Date
___ Cohabiting	____________	Date
___ Separated	____________	Date
___ Divorced	____________	Date
___ Widowed	____________	Date
___ Other	____________	

Number of Prior Marriages: ____________

Dates: ______________________

Children:

Age	Sex	At Home	When Left
___	___	___	___
___	___	___	___
___	___	___	___
___	___	___	___

Occupational History:

Patient:

______________________ (present/date)

______________________ (prior/date)

____

____

Spouse/partner:

______________________ (present/date)

______________________ (prior/date)

____

____

Education:

Patient: ______________________

Spouse/partner: ______________________

Religion: ______________________

Veteran Status: ______________________

2 INTRODUCTION

The interview should begin with a brief introduction and explanation of the purpose of the interview. A brief description of the presenting complaint should be obtained. In this section, a preliminary determination of the presence of panic attacks, phobic anxiety, and chronic worry should be made (as well as any medical difficulties or life circumstances that may be associated with the presenting complaints).

I will be asking you a number of questions about different areas of your life. First, I would like to get a general idea of what sorts of problems you have been having recently. What have they been?

____

____

____

If you had to identify one factor, what would you say is the <u>main</u> reason that brought you here today? (Record patient's response verbatim.)

____

____

In the past year, have you had any changes in or difficulties with:

Family/Relationships? ______________________________

____

____

Legal Matters/Police? ______________________________

____

____

Work/School? __________________________________

____

____

Financial? ____________________________________

____

____

Health (self)? __________________________________

____

Health (significant others)? __________________________

____

AFTER BRIEF INQUIRY:

Now I am going to ask you more questions about some specific kinds of problems that may or may not apply to you. We have already touched briefly on some of them, but now I would like to get more details.

PANIC DISORDER

I. INITIAL INQUIRY

1a. **Do you currently have times when you feel a sudden rush of intense fear or discomfort?**

YES ____ NO ____

If YES, skip to 2a.

b. If NO, **Have you ever had times when you have felt a sudden rush of intense fear or discomfort?**

YES ____ NO ____

If YES, **When was the most recent time this occurred?**

____

****

If YES to either 1a. or 1b., or uncertain, continue inquiry.
Otherwise skip to **AGORAPHOBIA** (p. 13).

****

2a. **Besides this current/most recent period of time when you have had these abrupt rushes of intense fear/discomfort, have there been other, separate periods of time when you experienced a sudden rush of intense fear or discomfort?**

YES ____ NO ____

If NO, skip to 3a.

b. **So prior to this current/most recent period of time when you have been experiencing these abrupt rushes of intense fear/discomfort, there was a considerable period of time when you were not having these rushes?**

YES ____ NO ____

If NO, skip to 3a.

c. **How much time separated these periods?; When did this/these separate period(s) occur?**

____

3a. **In what kinds of situation(s) do/did you have these feelings?; Where are/were you most likely to have these feelings?**

Current: ____

____

Past: ____

____

b. **Do/did you ever have these feelings come from "out of the blue," for no apparent reason, or in situations where you did not expect them to occur?**

Current: YES ____ NO ____
Past: YES ____ NO ____

4 PANIC DISORDER

If patient indicates the presence of unexpected panic symptoms, further inquiry is necessary to determine if these symptoms occur in a number of situational contexts or whether the symptoms are circumscribed to a particular type of situation (as can occur in Social or Specific Phobia).

4. **How long does/did it usually take for the rush of fear/discomfort to reach its peak level?**

Current:	________	minutes
Past:	________	minutes

5. **How long does/did the fear/discomfort usually last at its peak level?**

Current:	________	minutes
Past:	________	minutes

****

If no evidence of unexpected (uncued) panic attacks,
Skip to **AGORAPHOBIA** (p. 13).

****

II. SYMPTOM RATINGS

In this section rate symptoms only for panic attacks that occur **UNEXPECTEDLY**, in a variety of situations. Panic symptoms that are limited to a single stimulus (e.g., enclosed places or heights, social situations, obsessional content, etc.) should not be rated here.

In mixed or uncertain cases, ratings can be completed in this section.

Rate the severity of each symptom that is typical of the most recent period of attacks and, when appropriate, what characterized a typical attack in a separate past episode of disturbance. If a symptom is experienced during only some attacks (i.e., does not typically occur during an attack), enclose the rating in parentheses.

DSM-IV defines a panic attack as a discrete period of intense fear or discomfort, in which at least 4 of the symptoms listed below developed abruptly and reached a peak within 10 minutes. If typical attacks do not include 4 symptoms, determine if any attack has included 4 symptoms.

Use the following inquiry when rating symptoms:

CURRENT EPISODE:

1) **During this current period of attacks, do you usually experience_____ during the attacks?**

2) **How distressing/severe is the symptom to you?** If there is any doubt about whether the symptom is typical, ask: **Do you experience this nearly every time you have an attack?**

PAST EPISODE:

1) **During that period of time in __________ (years), did you usually experience ________ during the attacks?**

2) **How distressing/severe was the symptom to you?**; If there is any doubt about whether the symptom is typical, ask: **Did you experience this nearly every time you had an attack?**

1. Rate the severity of typical symptoms using the following scale:

0----------1----------2----------3----------4----------5----------6----------7----------8
None Mild Moderate Severe Very severe

	CURRENT FULL	CURRENT LSA	COMMENTS	PAST FULL	PAST LSA
a. Palpitations, pounding heart, or accelerated heart rate	___	___	___________	___	___
b. Sweating	___	___	___________	___	___
c. Trembling or shaking	___	___	___________	___	___
d. Shortness of breath or smothering sensations	___	___	___________	___	___
e. Feeling of choking	___	___	___________	___	___
f. Chest pain or discomfort	___	___	___________	___	___
g. Nausea or stomach distress	___	___	___________	___	___
h. Chills or hot flushes	___	___	___________	___	___
i. Dizziness, unsteady feelings, lightheadedness, or faintness	___	___	___________	___	___
j. Feelings of unreality or being detached from oneself	___	___	___________	___	___
k. Numbing or tingling sensations	___	___	___________	___	___
l. Fear of dying	___	___	___________	___	___
m. Fear of going crazy	___	___	___________	___	___
n. Fear of doing something uncontrolled	___	___	___________	___	___

2a. If the patient reports 4 or more symptoms per typical attack, ask:

Do/did you have periods (attacks/spells) when you have/had a sudden, unexpected rush of fear/discomfort that is/was accompanied by only one or two of these symptoms?

Current: YES ___ NO ___
Past: YES ___ NO ___

If YES, go back and rate severity of symptoms under Limited Symptom Attack (LSA) column.

b. If the patient reports less than 4 symptoms per typical attack, ask:

Do/did you have periods (attacks/spells) when you have/had a sudden, unexpected rush of fear/discomfort that is/was accompanied by four or more of these symptoms?

Current: YES ___ NO ___
Past: YES ___ NO ___

If YES, go back and rate severity of symptoms under Full Attack (FULL) column, switching ratings for typical, recent panic attacks to the Limited Symptom Attack (LSA) column.

III. CURRENT EPISODE

If evidence of a discrete past episode, preface inquiry in this section with: **Now I want to ask you a series of questions about this current period of panic attacks that began roughly in** __________ (specify month/year).

1a. **How many panic attacks have you had in the past month?**

________ Full ________ Limited

6 PANIC DISORDER

b. **How many panic attacks have you had in the past 6 months?**

_______ Full _______ Limited

2a. **In the last month, how much have you been worried about, or how apprehensive have you been of having another panic attack?**

Rating: __________

0---------1----------2---------3----------4----------5----------6---------7----------8

0	2	4	6	8
No worry/ No apprehension	Rarely worried/ Mild apprehension	Occasionally worried/ Moderate apprehension	Frequently worried/ Severe apprehension	Constantly worried/ Extreme apprehension

If no evidence of persistent concern/worry about panic over past month ask, **Since your first attack, has there been a period of a month a more when you were worried that you might have more attacks?**

YES ____ NO ____

If YES, **when was this?**

FROM __________ TO __________

b. **Specifically, what types of things do you anticipate happening as the result of the attacks?** (Inquire about immediate and long-term consequences.)

____

____

c. **Have the attacks caused you to change your behavior/lifestyle in any way?**

YES ____ NO ____

If YES, **how so?** ____

____

Situational avoidance (i.e., agoraphobia):

____

Interoceptive sensitivity/avoidance (e.g., physical exertion, sex, caffeine, expressing strong emotions, hot places, thrilling movies, activities that heighten awareness of bodily sensations):

____

Safety signals (e.g., medications, people, access to telephones/car):

____

Distraction (loud music, keeping TV on, staying involved in activities):

____

Lifestyle changes (e.g., reduction in "stressful" activities):

____

3. **In what ways have the panics interfered with your life (e.g., daily routine, job, social activities)?; How much are you bothered about having the attacks?**

____

____

Rate interference: __________ distress: __________

0----------1----------2----------3----------4----------5----------6----------7----------8
None Mild Moderate Severe Very severe

4a. **Can you recall your first panic attack that began this current period of attacks?**

YES ____ NO ____

If YES, **When did it happen?** __________ Month __________ Year

b. **Were you under any type of stress during this time?**

YES ____ NO ____

What was happening in your life at the time?

____

____

Were you experiencing any difficulties or changes in:

(1) **Family/relationships?** ______________________________

(2) **Work/school?** ______________________________

(3) **Finances?** ______________________________

(4) **Legal matters?** ______________________________

(5) **Health** (self/others)? ______________________________

c. **On the day of this first attack, were you taking any type of drug?** (Include alcohol/caffeine.)

YES ____ NO ____

If YES, specify type/amount: ______________________________

5. **Over this entire current period of time when you've been having the attacks, have you been regularly taking any types of drugs?**

YES ____ NO ____

Specify (type; amount; dates of use): ______________________________

____

6. **During this current period of time when you've been having the attacks, have you had any physical condition such as inner ear problems, mitral valve prolapse, pregnancy, hyperthyroidism, hypoglycemia?**

YES ____ NO ____

Specify (type; date of onset/remission): ______________________________

____

7. **For this current period of time when you've been having the attacks, when did the panic attacks become a problem in that they occurred regularly and/or you became very worried or anxious about having more attacks, or the attacks caused a change in your behavior in some way?** (Note: if patient is vague in date of onset, attempt to ascertain more specific information, e.g., by linking onset to objective life events.)

____

Date of Onset: __________ Month __________ Year

8. **Besides this current period of panic attacks, have there been other, separate periods of time before this when you have had these attacks?**

YES ___ NO ___

If YES, go back and ask 2b. and 2c. from INITIAL INQUIRY (p. 3).

If NO, skip to RESEARCH (p. 11, optional) or AGORAPHOBIA (p. 13).

IV. PAST EPISODE(S)

Now I want to ask you a series of questions about the past period of attacks that began roughly in _________ and ended roughly in _________ (specify months/years).

List dates (onset/remission) corresponding to period(s) of inquiry:

Past Episode #1: FROM __________ TO __________
Past Episode #2: FROM __________ TO __________

1. **During that period of time in _______** (years), **how many panic attacks did you typically have per month?**

Past Episode #1: _______ Full _______ Limited
Past Episode #2: _______ Full _______ Limited

2a. **During that period of time in _______** (years), **how much were you worried about, or how apprehensive were you of having another panic attack?**

0----------1----------2----------3----------4----------5----------6----------7----------8

0	2	4	6	8
No worry/ No apprehension	Rarely worried Mild apprehension	Occasionally worried Moderate apprehension	Frequently worried Severe apprehension	Constantly worried Extreme apprehension

Past Episode #1: _______
Past Episode #2: _______

If no evidence of persistent concern/worry over period ask, **Was there ever a period of a month a more during this time when you were worried that you might have more attacks?**

#1: YES ___ NO ___
#2: YES ___ NO ___

If YES, **when was this?**

#1: FROM __________ TO __________
#2: FROM __________ TO __________

b. **Specifically, what types of things did you anticipate happening as the result of the attacks?** (Inquire about immediate and long-term consequences.)

#1: ____________________

#2: ____________________

c. **Did the attacks cause you to change your behavior/lifestyle in any way?**

#1: YES ___ NO ___
#2: YES ___ NO ___

If YES, **how so?** #1: ____________________

#2: ____________________

Situational avoidance (i.e., agoraphobia):

____

Interoceptive sensitivity/avoidance (e.g., physical exertion, caffeine, expressing strong emotions, hot places, thrilling movies, activities that heighten awareness of bodily sensations):

____

Safety signals (e.g., medications, people, access to telephones/car):

____

Distraction (loud music, keeping TV on, staying involved in activities):

____

Lifestyle changes (e.g., reduction in "stressful" activities):

____

3. **In what ways did the panics interfere with your life (e.g., daily routine, job, social activities)?; How much were you bothered about having the attacks?**

#1: ____________________

#2: ____________________

#1: Rate interference: ________ distress: ________
#2: Rate interference: ________ distress: ________

0---------1----------2----------3----------4----------5----------6----------7----------8
None Mild Moderate Severe Very Severe

4a. **Can you recall your first panic attack that began the period of attacks in** ________ (year)?

#1: YES ___ NO ___
#2: YES ___ NO ___

If YES, **When did it happen?**

#1: ________ Month ________ Year
#2: ________ Month ________ Year

b. **Were you under any type of stress during this time?**

#1: YES ___ NO ___
#2: YES ___ NO ___

What was happening in your life at the time?

#1: ______________________________

#2: ______________________________

Were you experiencing any difficulties or changes in:

(1) **Family/relationships?** #1: ______________________________

#2: ______________________________

(2) **Work/school?** #1: ______________________________

#2: ______________________________

(3) **Finances?** #1: ______________________________

#2: ______________________________

(4) **Legal matters?** #1: ______________________________

#2: ______________________________

(5) **Health** (self/others)? #1: ______________________________

#2: ______________________________

c. **On the day of this first attack, were you taking any type of drug?** (Include alcohol/caffeine.)

#1: YES ____ NO ____
#2: YES ____ NO ____

If YES, specify type/amount: ______________________________

5. **During the period of time when you were having the attacks in** ________ (years), **were you regularly taking any types of drugs?**

#1: YES ____ NO ____
#2: YES ____ NO ____

Specify (type; amount; dates of use): ______________________________

____

6. **During the period of time when you were having the attacks in** ________ (years), **did you have any physical condition such as inner ear problems, mitral valve prolapse, pregnancy, hyperthyroidism, hypoglycemia?**

#1: YES ____ NO ____
#2: YES ____ NO ____

Specify (type; date of onset/remission): ______________________________

____

7. **During that period of time in ________ (years), when did the panic attacks become a problem in that they occurred regularly and/or you became very worried or anxious about having more attacks, or the attacks caused a change in your behavior in some way?** (Note: if patient is vague in date of onset, attempt to ascertain more specific information, e.g., by linking onset to objective life events.)

____

Date of Onset: #1: __________ Month __________ Year
#2: __________ Month __________ Year

8a. **When were the attacks no longer a problem, in that they stopped occurring and you were no longer worried or anxious about having more attacks?**

____

Date of remission: #1: __________ Month __________ Year
#2: __________ Month __________ Year

b. **Can you recall any reasons why the attacks stopped occurring or why you were no longer worried about them?**

#1: ____

#2: ____

9. **Prior to/after this past period of panic attacks, have there been other, separate periods of time that we haven't covered when you were having these attacks?**

YES ____ NO ____

If YES, ascertain whether a separate period of disturbance has existed of unexpected panic attacks (perhaps using items from INITIAL INQUIRY); if so, readminister items in PAST EPISODE for Past Episode #2.

If NO, continue to RESEARCH (optional) or skip to AGORAPHOBIA (p. 13).

V. RESEARCH

Inquiry should pertain to current episode of disturbance.

1. **What types of things seem to trigger the attacks?** [Inquire about internal (thoughts, sensations, images) and external (feared situations, situations that elicit heightened self-focused attention, physical effects of various activities such as caffeine, exercise, etc.) triggers.]

____

____

____

2. **When a panic attack occurs, how do you handle it?**

____

____

____

3. **Did you ever experience similar feelings, perhaps milder, when you were a child?**

YES ____ NO ____

If YES, specify dates and nature (situations, frequency, symptoms) of experiences:

____

____

4. **Have there been times when you awoke from sleep in a panic?**

YES ____ NO ____

If YES, ask:

a. **When in your sleep does this happen?**

____

b. **Does the panic usually occur shortly after you have fallen asleep, after you have been asleep for a while (e.g., middle of the night), or towards the morning near the time you'll be waking up?**

____

c. **Does the panic attack wake you from your sleep, or does the panic usually occur moments after you have awakened?**

____

____

If patient appears to experience nocturnal panics, ask:

d. **When did this occur?**

FROM ________ TO ________

e. **How often does/did this occur?**

____________ per week/month

AGORAPHOBIA

I. INITIAL INQUIRY

1a. **Do you currently feel panicky in any situations or avoid them because you might feel panicky?**

YES ____ NO ____

If YES, skip to 2a.

b. If NO, **Have you ever felt panicky in any situations or avoided them because of panic?**

YES ____ NO ____

If NO, continue to 1c.

When was the most recent time this occurred?

____

Skip to 2a.

c. **Are you currently apprehensive about entering situations due to the fear that you may develop such symptoms as diarrhea, vomiting, dizziness, etc.?**

YES ____ NO ____

If NO, continue to 1d.

What symptoms do you fear might arise in these situations?

____

Skip to 2a.

d. **Have you ever been apprehensive about entering situations due to the fear that you may develop such symptoms as diarrhea, vomiting, dizziness, etc.?**

YES ____ NO ____

If YES, **What symptoms did you fear might arise in these situations?**

____

When was the most recent time this occurred?

____

****

If NO to all of above and no history of Panic Disorder,
skip to **SOCIAL PHOBIA** (p. 18)

****

2a. **Besides this current/most recent period of time when you have been apprehensive of or avoided situations, have there been other, separate periods of time when you were apprehensive or avoided situations due to these feelings?**

YES ____ NO ____

If NO, skip to SITUATION RATINGS.

b. **So prior to this current/most recent period of time when you have been apprehensive of or avoided situations, there was a considerable period of time when you felt comfortable entering these situations?**

YES ____ NO ____

If NO, skip to SITUATION RATINGS.

c. **How much time separated these periods?; When did this/these separate period(s) occur?**

____

II. SITUATION RATINGS

Note: If existence of current or past panic disorder, obtain CURRENT and PAST agoraphobic situation ratings. If patient only reports a past episode of panic disorder, obtain CURRENT and PAST agoraphobic situation ratings (beginning with ratings for past agoraphobia). Ratings should pertain only to the anticipation of panic or other symptoms (e.g., diarrhea). Apprehension/avoidance due to other conditions (e.g., specific or social phobia) should be rated "0."

Use the following inquiry when rating situations:

How apprehensive are/were you to enter this situation?; How often do/did you avoid this situation?; Does/did having someone with you make a difference in terms of how comfortable you feel/felt in these situations?

0-----------1-----------2-----------3-----------4-----------5-----------6-----------7-----------8

0	2	4	6	8
No avoidance or escape/No apprehension	Occasional avoidance or escape/Mild apprehension	Moderate: may enter alone Moderate apprehension	Severe: rarely alone; must be accompanied/ Severe apprehension	Very Severe: never enters even with safe person/Very severe apprehension

	CURRENT			PAST	
	APPRE-HENSION	AVOID	COMMENTS	APPRE-HENSION	AVOID
a. Driving:					
Local	____	____	________	____	____
Long distance; interstate	____	____	________	____	____
b. Riding in car	____	____	________	____	____
c. Grocery stores	____	____	________	____	____
d. Malls	____	____	________	____	____
e. Crowds	____	____	________	____	____
f. Public transportation (e.g., bus, train)	____	____	________	____	____
g. Air travel	____	____	________	____	____
h. Doctor/dentist visits	____	____	________	____	____
i. Hairdresser	____	____	________	____	____
j. Waiting in line	____	____	________	____	____
k. Taking walks	____	____	________	____	____
l. Bridges	____	____	________	____	____
m. Being at home alone	____	____	________	____	____
n. Being out of town	____	____	________	____	____
o. Movie theaters; arenas	____	____	________	____	____

	CURRENT			PAST	
	APPRE-HENSION	AVOID	COMMENTS	APPRE-HENSION	AVOID
p. Restaurants	____	____	__________	____	____
q. Church	____	____	__________	____	____
r. Enclosed places:					
Elevators	____	____	__________	____	____
Small rooms/tunnels	____	____	__________	____	____
s. Open spaces (e.g., parks, parking lots)	____	____	__________	____	____
t. Work	____	____	__________	____	____
u. Other: __________	____	____	__________	____	____
__________	____	____	__________	____	____

****

If no evidence of fear or avoidance of any of these situations is obtained,
Skip to **SOCIAL PHOBIA** (p. 18).

****

III. CURRENT EPISODE

If evidence of a discrete past episode, preface inquiry in this section with: **Now I want to ask you a series of questions about this <u>current</u> period of apprehension/avoidance of situations that began roughly in** _________ (specify month/year).

1. **Are there any sorts of things that you carry with you, or things that you do before going out that help you feel more comfortable?** [Inquire about safety signals such as medication bottles, cellular phones, having access to own car, books/printed coping instructions, drinks, materials relating to getting sick in public (e.g., paper towels).]

   ____

   ____

2. **In what ways has the apprehension/avoidance of these situations interfered with your life (e.g., daily routine, job, social activities)?**

   ____

   ____

   Rate interference: _________ distress: _________

   0----------1----------2----------3----------4----------5----------6----------7----------8
   None Mild Moderate Severe Very severe

3. **For this current period of time, when did the apprehension over entering these situations begin?** (Note: if patient is vague in date of onset, attempt to ascertain more specific information, e.g., by linking onset to objective life events, initial panic attack.)

   ____

Date of Onset: _________ Month _________ Year

4. **Besides this current period of time, have there been other, separate periods of time before this when you were apprehensive or avoided situations due to these feelings?**

YES ____ NO ____

If YES, go back and ask 2b. and 2c. from INITIAL INQUIRY (p. 13).

If NO, skip to SOCIAL PHOBIA (p. 18).

IV. PAST EPISODE(S)

Now I want to ask you a series of questions about the past period of apprehension/avoidance of situations that began roughly in ________ and ended roughly in ________ (specify months/years):

List dates (onset/remission) corresponding to period(s) of inquiry:

Past Episode #1: FROM ____________ TO ____________
Past Episode #2: FROM ____________ TO ____________

1. **Were there any sorts of things that you carried with you, or things that you did before going out that helped you feel more comfortable?**

#1: ____

#2: ____

2. **In what ways did the apprehension/avoidance of these situations interfere with your life (e.g., daily routine, job, social activities)?**

#1: ____

#2: ____

Rate distress/interference: #1: ____________
#2: ____________

0----------1----------2----------3----------4----------5----------6----------7----------8
None Mild Moderate Severe Very severe

3. **For that past period of time when you were apprehensive over entering situations, when did that begin?** (Note: if patient is vague in date of onset, attempt to ascertain more specific information, e.g., by linking onset to objective life events, initial panic attack.)

____

Date of Onset: #1: ____________ Month ____________ Year
#2: ____________ Month ____________ Year

4a. **When was the apprehension/avoidance of situations no longer a problem, in that you felt comfortable entering all of these situations?**

____

Date of remission: #1: ____________ Month ____________ Year
#2: ____________ Month ____________ Year

b. **Can you recall any reasons why you began to feel comfortable entering these situations again?**

#1: ____

#2: ____

5. **Prior to/after this past period, have there been other, separate periods of time that we haven't covered when you were apprehensive or avoided situations due to these feelings?**

YES ____ NO ____

If YES, ascertain whether a separate period of disturbance has existed of agoraphobic avoidance (perhaps using items from INITIAL INQUIRY); if so, readminister items for Past Episode #2.

If NO, skip to SOCIAL PHOBIA (p. 18).

SOCIAL PHOBIA

I. INITIAL INQUIRY

1a. **Currently, in social situations where you might be observed or evaluated by others or when you are meeting new people, do you feel fearful, anxious, or nervous?**

YES ____ NO ____

b. **Currently, are you overly concerned that you may do and/or say something that might embarrass or humiliate yourself in front of others, or that others may think badly of you?**

YES ____ NO ____

If NO to 1a. and 1b., continue to 1c.

If YES to either 1a. or 1b., skip to 2a.

c. **Have you ever been anxious in social situations or were you ever overly concerned about embarrassing or humiliating yourself in front of others?**

YES ____ NO ____

If NO, skip to 3.

When was the most recent time this occurred?

____

2a. **Besides this current/most recent period of time when you felt anxious in social situations, have there been other, separate periods of time when you were anxious in social situations or were overly concerned about embarrassing or humiliating yourself in front of others?**

YES ____ NO ____

If NO, skip to 3.

b. **So prior to this current/most recent period of time when you have felt anxious in social situations, there was a considerable period of time when you felt comfortable in these situations?**

YES ____ NO ____

If NO, skip to 3.

c. **How much time separated these periods?; When did this/these separate period(s) occur?**

____

3. **I am going to describe some situations of this type and ask how you would feel in each situation and to what extent you avoid these situations.**

If patient does not report current or past social anxiety (i.e., NO to 1a., 1b., and 1c.), inquire about CURRENT situations only. If patient reports current or past social anxiety (i.e., YES to either 1a., 1b., 1c., or 2a.), inquire about both CURRENT and PAST situations. Particularly if there is evidence of separate episodes, inquire for the presence of prior discrete episodes of disturbance (e.g., "**Since the fear began, have there been periods of time when you were not bothered by it?**"). Use space for comments to record other clinically useful information (e.g., frequency with which feared situation arises).

For each situation, make separate ratings for level of fear and degree of avoidance using the following scale:

0---------1---------2----------3----------4----------5----------6----------7----------8

No fear/ Never avoids | Mild fear/ Rarely avoids | Moderate fear/ Sometimes avoids | Severe fear/ Often avoids | Very severe fear/ Always avoids

CURRENT: **Currently, are you anxious in or feel a need to avoid:**
PAST: **Have you ever been anxious in or felt a need to avoid:**

	CURRENT			PAST	
	FEAR	AVOID	COMMENTS	FEAR	AVOID
a. Parties	____	____	____________	____	____
b. Participating at meetings/classes	____	____	____________	____	____
c. Talking in front of a group/formal speaking	____	____	____________	____	____
d. Speaking with unfamiliar people	____	____	____________	____	____
e. Eating in public	____	____	____________	____	____
f. Using public restrooms	____	____	____________	____	____
g. Writing in public (signing checks, filling out forms)	____	____	____________	____	____
h. Dating situations	____	____	____________	____	____
i. Talking to persons in authority	____	____	____________	____	____
j. Being assertive, e.g.:					
-Refusing unreasonable requests	____	____	____________	____	____
-Asking others to change their behavior	____	____	____________	____	____
k. Initiating a conversation	____	____	____________	____	____
l. Maintaining a conversation	____	____	____________	____	____
m. Other ____________________	____	____	____________	____	____
____________________	____	____	____________	____	____

****

If no evidence of fear/avoidance is obtained,
Skip to **GENERALIZED ANXIETY DISORDER** (p. 23).

****

II. CURRENT EPISODE

If evidence of a discrete past episode, preface inquiry in this section with: **Now I want to ask you a series of questions about your <u>current</u> anxiety in social situations that began roughly in** _________ (specify month/year).

Complete for current episode of social anxiety that is potentially of clinical severity:

A. List most problematic situations: ______________________________________

1. **What are you concerned will happen in these situations?** ______________________

____

2. **Do you experience the anxiety nearly every time you encounter** ________**?**

YES ____ NO ____

3. **Does the anxiety occur as soon as you enter the situations or are about to enter the situations, or is the anxiety sometimes delayed or unexpected?**

IMMEDIATE ____ DELAYED ____

4a. **Are you anxious about these situations because you are afraid that you will have an unexpected panic attack?**

YES ____ NO ____

If YES,

b. **Other than times when you are exposed to ____________, have you experienced an unexpected rush of fear/anxiety?**

YES ____ NO ____

If YES, **where has this occurred?** ____

If YES to 4a. or 4b., consider whether fear could be subsumed into panic disorder.

5a. **In what ways have these fears interfered with your life (e.g., daily routine, job, social activities)?; How much are you bothered by these fears?**

____

____

b. **Has your current job or educational attainment been influenced by the fears?**

____

____

Rate interference: __________ distress: __________

0----------1----------2----------3----------4----------5----------6----------7----------8

None Mild Moderate Severe Very severe

6a. **When did anxiety about __________ begin to be a problem in that it caused a lot of distress or interference with your life?** (Note: if patient is vague in date of onset, attempt to ascertain more specific information, e.g., by linking onset to objective life events.)

____

Date of Onset: __________ Month __________ Year

b. **Can you recall anything that might have contributed to you feeling anxious about social situations?**

____

____

7. **Besides this current period of anxiety in social situations, have there been other, separate periods of time before this when you have had the same problems?**

YES ____ NO ____

If YES, go back and ask 2b. and 2c. from INITIAL INQUIRY (p. 18).

If NO, skip to RESEARCH (p. 22, optional) or GENERALIZED ANXIETY DISORDER (p. 23)

III. PAST EPISODES

Now I want to ask you a series of questions about anxiety in social situations that began roughly in _________ and ended roughly in _________ (specify months/years).

Complete for past episode of social anxiety that was potentially of clinical severity:

A. List most problematic situations: ______________________________

1. **What were you concerned would happen in these situations?** ______________________________

____

2. **Did you experience the anxiety nearly every time you encountered ________?**

YES ____ NO ____

3. **Did the anxiety occur as soon as you entered the situations or were about to enter the situations, or was the anxiety sometimes delayed or unexpected?**

IMMEDIATE ____ DELAYED ____

4a. **Were you anxious about these situations because you were afraid that you would have an unexpected panic attack?**

YES ____ NO ____

If YES,

b. **Other than times when you were exposed to __________, had you experienced an unexpected rush of fear/anxiety?**

YES ____ NO ____

If YES, **where did that occur?** ______________________________

If YES to 4a. or 4b., consider whether fear could be subsumed into panic disorder.

5. **In what ways did these fears interfere with your life (e.g., daily routine, job, social activities)?; How much were you bothered by these fears?**

____

____

Rate interference: __________ distress: __________

0----------1----------2----------3----------4----------5----------6----------7----------8
None . Mild Moderate Severe Very severe

6a. **When did the anxiety about _________ begin to be a problem in that it caused a lot of distress or interference with your life?** (Note: if patient is vague in date of onset, attempt to ascertain more specific information, e.g., by linking onset to objective life events.)

____

Date of Onset: __________ Month __________ Year

b. **Can you recall anything that might have contributed to you feeling anxious about social situations?**

____

7a. **When was anxiety about ________ no longer a problem in that you were comfortable with __________, or it no longer caused a lot of distress or interference with your life?**

____

Date of Remission: ___________ Month ___________ Year

b. **Can you recall any reasons why you were no longer anxious about these situations?**

____

8. **Prior to/after this past period of anxiety in social situations, have there been other, separate periods of time that we haven't covered when you have had the same problems?**

YES ____ NO ____

If YES, go back and ask 2b. and 2c. from INITIAL INQUIRY (p. 18).

If NO, continue to RESEARCH (optional) or skip to GENERALIZED ANXIETY DISORDER (p. 23).

IV. RESEARCH

Inquiry should pertain to current episodes of disturbance.

A. PANIC ATTACK SYMPTOMS

1. List situation(s) being rated: ____

Do you experience ____________ when you encounter __________?

0----------1----------2----------3----------4----------5----------6----------7----------8

None Mild Moderate Severe Very severe

1. Palpitations, pounding heart, or accelerated heart rate ___
2. Sweating ___
3. Trembling or shaking ___
4. Shortness of breath or smothering sensations ___
5. Feeling of choking ___
6. Chest pain or discomfort ___
7. Nausea or stomach distress ___
8. Chills, hot flushes, or blushing ___
9. Dizziness, unsteady feelings, lightheadedness, or faintness ___
10. Feelings of unreality or being detached from oneself ___
11. Numbing or tingling sensations ___
12. Fear of dying ___
13. Fear of going crazy ___
14. Fear of doing something uncontrolled ___
15. Tics or spasms ___

GENERALIZED ANXIETY DISORDER

I. INITIAL INQUIRY

1a. **Over the last several months, have you been continually worried or anxious about a number of events or activities in your daily life?**

YES ____ NO ____

If NO, skip to 1b.

What kinds of things do you worry about? ______________________________

____

Skip to 2a.

b. **Have you ever experienced an extended period when you were continually worried or anxious about a number of events or activities in your daily life?**

YES ____ NO ____

If NO, skip to 3.

What kinds of things did you worry about? ______________________________

____

When was the most recent time this occurred? ______________________________

2a. **Besides this current/most recent period of time when you have been persistently worried about different areas of your life, have there been other, separate periods of time when you were continually worried about a number of life matters?**

YES ____ NO ____

If NO, skip to 3.

b. **So prior to this current/most recent period of time when you were worried about different areas of your life, there was a considerable period of time when you were not having these persistent worries?**

YES ____ NO ____

c. **How much time separated these periods?; When did this/these separate period(s) occur?**

____

3. **Now I want to ask you a series of questions about worry over the following areas of life:**

If patient does not report current or past persistent worry (i.e., NO to 1a. and 1b.), inquire about CURRENT areas of worry only. If patient reports current or past persistent worry, (i.e., YES to either 1a. or 1b.), inquire about both CURRENT and PAST areas of worry. Particularly if there is evidence of separate episodes, inquire for the presence of prior discrete episodes of disturbance (e.g., "**Since these worries began, have there been periods of time when you were not bothered by them?**"). Use the space below each general worry area to record the specific content of the patient's worry (including information obtained previously from items 1a. and 1b.). Further inquiry will often be necessary to determine whether areas of worry reported by patient are unrelated to a co-occurring Axis I disorder. If it is determined that an area of worry can be subsumed totally by another Axis I disorder, rate this area as "0." Use comment section to record clinically useful information (e.g., data pertaining to the discreteness of episodes, co-existing disorder with which the area of worry is related).

For each area of worry, make separate ratings of excessiveness (i.e., frequency and intensity) and perceived uncontrollability using the scales and suggested queries below.

EXCESSIVENESS:

0	1	2	3	4	5	6	7	8
No worry/ No tension		Rarely worried/Mild tension		Occasionally worried/Moderate tension		Frequently worried/Severe tension		Constantly worried/Extreme tension

CONTROLLABILITY:

0	1	2	3	4	5	6	7	8
Never/ No difficulty		Rarely/ Slight difficulty		Occasionally/ Moderate difficulty		Frequently/ Marked difficulty		Constantly/ Extreme difficulty

EXCESSIVENESS:

How often do/did you worry about ________?; If things are/were going well, do/did you still worry about ________?; How much tension and anxiety does/did the worry about __________ produce?

UNCONTROLLABILITY:

Do/did you find it hard to control the worry about _________ in that it is/was difficult to stop worrying about it?; Is/was the worry about _________ hard to control in that it will/would come into your mind when you are/were trying to focus on something else?

	CURRENT			PAST	
	EXCESS	CONTROL	COMMENTS	EXCESS	CONTROL
a. Minor matters (e.g., punctuality, small repairs) ________________	___	___	________________	___	___
b. Work/school ________________	___	___	________________	___	___
c. Family ________________	___	___	________________	___	___
d. Finances ________________	___	___	________________	___	___
e. Social/interpersonal ________________	___	___	________________	___	___
f. Health (self) ________________	___	___	________________	___	___
g. Health (significant others) ________________	___	___	________________	___	___
h. Community/world affairs ________________	___	___	________________	___	___

	CURRENT		COMMENTS	PAST	
	EXCESS	CONTROL		EXCESS	CONTROL
i. Other					
______________________	___	___	______________	___	___
j. Other					
______________________	___	___	______________	___	___

****

If no evidence of excessive/uncontrollable worry is obtained,
Skip to **OBSESSIVE-COMPULSIVE DISORDER** (p. 31).

****

II. CURRENT EPISODE

If evidence of a discrete past episode, preface inquiry in this section with: **Now I want to ask you a series of questions about this <u>current</u> period of worry over these areas that began roughly in** __________ (specify month/year).

List principal topics of worry: ____

____

1. **During the past 6 months, have you been bothered these worries more days than not?**

   YES ___ NO ___

2. **On an average day over the past month, what percentage of the day did you feel worried?**

   __________ %

3. **Specifically, what types of things do you worry might happen regarding** ______________ (inquire for each principal area of worry)?

   ____

   ____

   ____

4. **During the past 6 months, have you often experienced** _________ **when you worried?; Has** _________ **been present more days than not over the past 6 months?** (Do not record symptoms that are associated with other conditions such as panic, social anxiety, etc.)

   0----------1----------2----------3----------4----------5----------6----------7----------8
   None Mild Moderate Severe Very severe

	SEVERITY	MORE DAYS THAN NOT
a. restlessness; feeling keyed up or on edge	___	Y N
b. being easily fatigued	___	Y N
c. difficulty concentrating or mind going blank	___	Y N
d. irritability	___	Y N
e. muscle tension	___	Y N
f. difficulty falling/staying asleep; restless/unsatisfying sleep	___	Y N

5. **In what ways have these worries and the tension/anxiety associated with them interfered with your life (e.g., daily routine, job, social activities)?; How much are you bothered about having these worries?**

____

____

Rate interference: __________ distress: __________

0---------1----------2----------3----------4----------5----------6----------7----------8
None Mild Moderate Severe Very severe

6. **Over this entire current period of time when you've been having these worries and ongoing feelings of tension/anxiety, have you been regularly taking any types of drugs** (e.g., drugs of abuse, medication)**?**

YES ____ NO ____

Specify (type; amount; dates of use): ______________________________

____

7. **During this current period of time when you've been having the worries and ongoing feelings of tension/anxiety, have you had any physical condition** (e.g., hyperthyroidism)**?**

YES ____ NO ____

Specify (type; date of onset/remission): ______________________________

____

8a. **For this current period of time, when did these worries and symptoms of tension/anxiety become a problem in that they occurred persistently, you were bothered by the worry or symptoms and found them hard to control, or they interfered with your life in some way?** (Note: if patient is vague in date of onset, attempt to ascertain more specific information, e.g., by linking onset to objective life events.)

____

Date of Onset: __________ Month __________ Year

b. **Can you recall anything that might have led to this problem?** ______________

____

____

c. **Were you under any type of stress during this time?**

YES ____ NO ____

What was happening in your life at the time?

____

____

Were you experiencing any difficulties or changes in:

(1) **Family/relationships?** ______________________________

(2) **Work/school?** ____________________

(3) **Finances?** ____________________

(4) **Legal matters?** ____________________

(5) **Health** (self/others)? ____________________

9. **Besides this current period of worry and tension/anxiety, have there been other, separate periods of time before this when you have had the same problems?**

YES ____ NO ____

If YES, go back and ask 2b. and 2c. from INITIAL INQUIRY (p. 23).

If NO, skip to RESEARCH (p. 29, optional) or OBSESSIVE-COMPULSIVE DISORDER (p. 31)

III. PAST EPISODE

Now I want to ask you a series of questions about the past period of worry over these areas that been roughly in ________ and ended roughly in ________ (specify months/years).

List principal topics of worry: ____________________

____

1. **During that time, were you bothered these worries more days than not for at least 6 months?**

YES ____ NO ____

2. **On an average day during these period, what percentage of the day did you feel worried?**

________ %

3. **Specifically, what types of things did you worry might happen regarding** ____________ (inquire for each principal area of worry)?

____

____

____

4. **During that time, did you often experience ________ when you worried?; Did you experience ________ more days than not for at least 6 months during that time?** (Do not record symptoms that were associated with other conditions such as panic, social anxiety, etc.)

0----------1----------2----------3----------4----------5----------6----------7----------8

None Mild Moderate Severe Very severe

	SEVERITY	MORE DAYS THAN NOT
a. restlessness; feeling keyed up or on edge	____	Y N
b. being easily fatigued	____	Y N
c. difficulty concentrating or mind going blank	____	Y N
d. irritability	____	Y N
e. muscle tension	____	Y N
f. difficulty falling/staying asleep; restless/unsatisfying sleep	____	Y N

5. **In what ways did these worries and the tension/anxiety associated with them interfere with your life (e.g., daily routine, job, social activities)?; How much were you bothered about having these worries?**

____

____

Rate interference: __________ distress: __________

0----------1----------2----------3----------4----------5----------6----------7----------8
None Mild Moderate Severe Very severe

6. **During that period of time in _______ (years) when you were having these worries and ongoing feelings of tension/anxiety, were you regularly taking any types of drugs** (e.g., drugs of abuse, medication)?

YES ____ NO ____

Specify (type; amount; dates of use): ______________________________

____

7. **During that period of time in _______ (years) when you were having the worries and ongoing feelings of tension/anxiety, did you have any physical condition** (e.g., hyperthyroidism)?

YES ____ NO ____

Specify (type; date of onset/remission): ______________________________

____

8a. **During that period of time in _______ (years), when did these worries and symptoms of tension/anxiety become a problem in that they occurred persistently, you were bothered by the worry or symptoms and found them hard to control, or they interfered with your life in some way?** (Note: if patient is vague in date of onset, attempt to ascertain more specific information, e.g., by linking onset to objective life events.)

____

Date of Onset: __________ Month __________ Year

b. **Can you recall anything that might have led to this problem?** ______________________

____

c. **Were you under any type of stress during this time?**

YES ____ NO ____

What was happening in your life at the time? ______________________________

____

____

Were you experiencing any difficulties or changes in:

(1) **Family/relationships?** ______________________________

(2) **Work/school?** ______________________________

(3) **Finances?** ______________________________

(4) **Legal matters?** ______________________________

(5) **Health** (self/others)? ______________________________

9a. **When was this no longer a problem, in that the worries and symptoms of tension/anxiety did not occur persistently, you weren't bothered by the worry or symptoms nor found them hard to control, and they did not interfere with your life?**

Date of Remission: __________ Month __________ Year

b. **Can you recall any reasons why these worries and symptoms of tension/anxiety were no longer a problem for you?**

____

____

10. **Prior to/after this past period of worry and tension/anxiety, have there been other, separate periods of time that we haven't covered when you have had the same problems?**

YES ____ NO ____

If YES, go back and ask 2b. and 2c. from INITIAL INQUIRY (p. 23).

If NO, continue to RESEARCH (optional) or skip to OBSESSIVE-COMPULSIVE DISORDER (p. 31).

IV. RESEARCH

Inquiry should pertain to current episode of disturbance.

List principal topics of worry: ______________________________

____

1a. **When a worry comes into your mind, what usually triggers it?** (Inquire about worry precipitants, e.g., situations, activities.)

____

____

b. **How often does a worry come into your mind for no apparent reason?**

____

____

Rate frequency of unprecipitated worry (per week): ________

0----------1----------2---------3----------4---------5----------6----------7----------8

Never | Rarely | Sometimes | Often | Very often/Always

2a. **Do your worries prompt you to do anything to reassure yourself or to reduce the anxiety/tension associated with the worry?** (Inquire about behaviors performed in response to the worry; e.g., checking, preventative actions, reassurance seeking, distraction.)

YES ____ NO ____

If YES, specify: ____

____

For each worry behavior noted:

b. **How often does a worry prompt you to engage in an action aimed at reassuring yourself or reducing your tension/anxiety?**

____

Rate frequency: Worry behavior #1 ____________________: ________
Worry behavior #2 ____________________: ________

0----------1----------2----------3----------4---------5----------6----------7----------8
Never Rarely Sometimes Often Very often/Always

3a. **Prior to the first time that this really became a problem** [refer to date of onset of first episode], **did you have a tendency to worry?**

YES ____ NO ____

b. If YES, **What are some examples showing this tendency** (e.g., reacting to stress more strongly than others; sleepless nights before exams, new jobs/school year)?

____

____

4a. **Can you remember having a tendency to worry when you were a child?**

YES ____ NO ____

b. If YES, **Can you identify any things that were going on in your life during childhood that contributed to your tendency to worry?** (Inquire about stressful life events, unstable family life, exposure to others' worry behaviors/mental illness, etc.)

YES ____ NO ____

If YES, specify: ____

____

OBSESSIVE-COMPULSIVE DISORDER

I. INITIAL INQUIRY

1a. **Currently, are you bothered by thoughts, images, or impulses that keep recurring to you that seem inappropriate or nonsensical but that you can't stop from coming into your mind?**

YES ____ NO ____

If YES, specify: ____

____

b. **Currently, do you feel driven to repeat some behavior or to repeat something in your mind over and over again to try to feel less uncomfortable?**

YES ____ NO ____

If YES, specify: ____

____

If NO to 1a. and 1b., continue to 1c. and 1d.

If YES to either 1a. or 1b., skip to 2a.

c. **Have you <u>ever</u> had a time when you were bothered by thoughts, images, or impulses that kept recurring to you that seemed inappropriate or nonsensical?**

YES ____ NO ____

If YES, specify: ____

____

d. **Have you <u>ever</u> felt driven to repeat some behavior or to repeat something in your mind over and over again to try to feel less uncomfortable?**

YES ____ NO ____

If YES, specify: ____

____

If NO to 1c. and 1d., skip to 3 (Obsessions & Compulsions Ratings).

When was the most recent time this occurred?

____

2a. **Besides this current/most recent period of time, have there been other, separate periods of time when you were bothered by such thoughts, images, impulses, or repetitive actions?**

YES ____ NO ____

If NO, skip to 3.

b. **So prior to this current/most recent period of time, there was a considerable period of time when you were not having these thoughts, images, impulses, and repetitive actions?**

YES ____ NO ____

c. **How much time separated these periods?; When did this/these separate period(s) occur?**

____

3. Obsessions and Compulsions Ratings

If patient does not report current or past obsessions and compulsions (i.e., NO to 1a. through 1d.), inquire about CURRENT obsessions and compulsions only. If patient reports current or past obsessions or compulsions (i.e., YES to 1a., 1b., 1c., or 1d.), inquire about both CURRENT and PAST obsessions and compulsions. Particularly if there is evidence of separate episodes, inquire for the presence of prior discrete episodes of disturbance (e.g., "**Since these thoughts/images/behaviors began, have there been periods of time when you were not bothered by them?**"). Use the space below each item to record the specific content and nature of the patient's obsessions and/or compulsions (including information obtained previously from items 1a. through 1d.). If it is determined that an item below can be better accounted for by another Axis I disorder, rate it "0." Use comment section to record clinically useful information (e.g., data pertaining to the discreteness of episodes, co-existing disorder with which the item is related).

OBSESSIONS:

For each obsession, make separate ratings of Persistence/Distress and Resistance using the scales and suggested queries below.

PERSISTENCE/DISTRESS:

How often does ________ enter your mind?; How distressing is it to you when ________ enters your mind?

0----------1----------2----------3----------4----------5----------6----------7----------8

0	2	4	6	8
Never/ No distress	Rarely/ Mild distress	Occasionally/ Moderate distress	Frequently/ Marked distress	Constantly/ Extreme distress

RESISTANCE:

How often do you attempt to get rid of ________ by ignoring, suppressing, or trying to neutralize it/them with some thought or action?

0----------1----------2----------3----------4----------5----------6----------7----------8

0	2	4	6	8
Never	Rarely	Occasionally	Frequently	Constantly

	CURRENT			PAST	
	PERSIST/ DISTRESS	RESIST	COMMENTS	PERSIST/ DISTRESS	RESIST
a. Doubting (e.g., locks, turning appliances off, completion/accuracy of tasks)	____	____	____________	____	____
b. Contamination (e.g., contracting germs from doorknobs, toilets, money, etc.)	____	____	____________	____	____
c. Nonsensical impulses (e.g., shouting/ undressing in public)	____	____	____________	____	____

	CURRENT			PAST	
	PERSIST/ DISTRESS	RESIST	COMMENTS	PERSIST/ DISTRESS	RESIST
d. Aggressive impulses (e.g., hurting self or others intentionally, destroying objects)	____	____	____________	____	____
e. Sexual (e.g., obscene thoughts or images)	____	____	____________	____	____
f. Religious/Satanic (e.g., blasphemous thoughts/impulses)	____	____	____________	____	____
g. Accidental harm to others (e.g., poisoning or hurting someone unknowingly)	____	____	____________	____	____
h. Horrific images (e.g., mutilated bodies)	____	____	____________	____	____
i. Nonsensical thoughts/images (e.g., numbers, letters, songs)	____	____	____________	____	____
j. Other	____	____	____________	____	____
k. Other	____	____	____________	____	____

COMPULSIONS:

For each compulsion, make ratings of Frequency using the scale and suggested queries below.

FREQUENCY:

How often are you driven to perform such actions as ______________________?

0----------1----------2----------3----------4----------5----------6----------7----------8

Never — Rarely — Occasionally — Frequently — Constantly

	CURRENT		PAST
	FREQ	COMMENTS	FREQ
a. Counting (e.g., certain letters or numbers, other objects in the environment)	____	____________	____

0----------1----------2----------3----------4----------5----------6----------7----------8
Never Rarely Occasionally Frequently Constantly

	CURRENT FREQ	COMMENTS	PAST FREQ
b. Checking (e.g., locks, appliances, driving routes, important papers, waste baskets) ______	____	______	____
c. Washing ______	____	______	____
d. Hoarding (e.g., newspapers, garbage, trivial items) ______	____	______	____
e. Internal repetition (e.g., phrases, words, prayers) ______	____	______	____
f. Adhering to certain rules or sequences (e.g., assuring symmetry, ritualistic acts, adhering to a specific routine for daily activities) ______	____	______	____
g. Other ______	____	______	____
h. Other ______	____	______	____

****

If no evidence of obsessions or compulsions is obtained,
Skip to **SPECIFIC PHOBIA** (p. 41).

****

II. CURRENT EPISODE

A. Obsessions

If no evidence of obsessions has been obtained, skip to Compulsions (p. 35)

If evidence of a discrete past episode, preface inquiry in this section with: **Now I want to ask you a series of questions about this current period of repetitive thoughts, images, or impulses that began roughly in** ________ (specify month/year).

List principal obsessions: 1: ______________________________

2: ______________________________

Inquire for each obsession:

1a. **On the average day over the past month, what percentage of the day were the thoughts/ impulses/images about _________ in your mind?**

#1: _________ % #2: _________ % Overall: _________ %

b. If uncertain, **Are these thoughts/impulses/images typically in your mind for at least an hour a day?**

YES ____ NO ____

2a. **While the thought/impulse/image about ________ is in your mind, how strongly do you believe that it is true** (0-100 scale where 0 = not at all and 100 = completely)?

#1: _________ % #2: _________ %

b. **For this current period of time when you've been bothered by these thoughts/images/impulses about __________, how strongly did you believe that they were true, even during times when they were not in your mind** (0-100 scale)?

#1: _________ % #2: _________ %

3. **How do these thoughts/images/impulses about ___________ come into your mind** (ascertain whether patient recognizes that obsessions are a product of his/her own mind)?

____

If evidence of thought insertion, **Are these thoughts/images/impulses ever imposed by something outside of you?**

YES ____ NO ____

If YES, specify ____

4. **In what way do these thoughts/images/impulses concern you?; What do you worry that having these thoughts/images/impulses might mean?**

____

____

B. Compulsions

If no evidence of compulsions has been obtained, skip to Current Episode (Obsessions & Compulsions; p. 36).

If evidence of a discrete past episode, preface inquiry in this section with: **Now I want to ask you a series of questions about this current period of repetitive behaviors or mental actions that began roughly in __________** (specify month/year).

List principal compulsions: 1: ____

2: ____

Inquire for each compulsion:

1a. **On the average day over the past month, what percentage of the day were you _______________?**

#1: _________ % #2: _________ % Overall: _________ %

b. If uncertain, **Do you typically spend at least an hour a day performing these behaviors/mental actions?**

YES ____ NO ____

2. **Do you feel that repeating these behaviors/mental actions doesn't make sense or takes up more time than is really necessary?**

YES ____ NO ____

Specify: ____________________

If NO, **At any time during this current period when you've been bothered by these behaviors/mental acts, did you feel that they didn't make sense or took up more time than necessary?**

YES ____ NO ____

Specify: ____________________

3a. **How often do you resist carrying out these behaviors/mental acts?**

____

b. **How anxious do you feel if you can't or don't carry out these acts?**

____

c. **What do you worry might happen if you don't carry out these acts?**

____

C. Current Episode (Obsessions and/or Compulsions)

1. **In what ways have these repetitive thoughts/images/impulses/behaviors interfered with your life (e.g., daily routine, job, social activities)?; How much are you bothered by these symptoms?**

____

____

Rate interference: __________ distress: __________

0----------1----------2----------3----------4----------5----------6----------7----------8
None Mild Moderate Severe Very severe

2. **Over this entire current period of time when you've been having these repetitive thoughts/images/impulses/behaviors, have you been regularly taking any types of drugs** (include drugs of abuse, medication)**?**

YES ____ NO ____

Specify (type; amount; dates of use): ____________________

____

3. **During this current period of time when you've been having the repetitive thoughts/images/impulses/behaviors, have you had any physical condition?**

YES ____ NO ____

Specify (type; date of onset/remission): ____________________

____

4a. **For this current period of time, when did these repetitive thoughts/images/impulses/behaviors become a problem in that they occurred persistently (over an hour per day), you were bothered by the symptoms, or they interfered with your life in some way?** (Note: if patient is vague in date of onset, attempt to ascertain more specific information, e.g., by linking onset to objective life events.)

____

Date of Onset: __________ Month __________ Year

b. **Can you recall anything that might have led to this problem?** __________

____

____

c. **Were you under any type of stress during this time?**

YES ___ NO ___

What was happening in your life at the time?

____

____

Were you experiencing any difficulties or changes in:

(1) **Family/relationships?** __________

(2) **Work/school?** __________

(3) **Finances?** __________

(4) **Legal matters?** __________

(5) **Health** (self/others)? __________

5. **Besides this current period of time when you've been having these repetitive thoughts/images/impulses/behaviors, have there been other, separate periods of time before this when you have had the same problems?**

YES ___ NO ___

If YES, go back and ask 2b. and 2c. from INITIAL INQUIRY (p. 31).

If NO, skip to SPECIFIC PHOBIA (p. 41).

III. PAST EPISODE

A. Obsessions

If no evidence of obsessions has been obtained, skip to Compulsions (p. 38)

Now I want to ask you a series of questions about the <u>past</u> period of repetitive thoughts, images, or impulses that began roughly in ________ and ended roughly in ________ (specify months/years).

List principal obsessions: 1: __________

2: __________

Inquire for each obsession:

1a. **On the average day during this period, what percentage of the day were the thoughts/impulses/images about ________ in your mind?**

#1: ________ % #2: ________ % Overall: ________ %

b. If uncertain, **Were these thoughts/impulses/images typically in your mind for at least an hour a day?**

YES ____ NO ____

2a. **While the thought/impulse/image about ________ was in your mind, how strongly did you believe that it was true** (0-100 scale where 0 = not at all and 100 = completely)?

#1: ________ % #2: ________ %

b. **During that period of time when you were bothered by these thoughts/images/impulses about ________, how strongly did you believe that they were true, even during times when they were not in your mind** (0-100 scale)?

#1: ________ % #2: ________ %

3. **How did these thoughts/images/impulses about ____________ come into your mind?** (Ascertain whether patient recognizes that obsessions are a product of his/her own mind.)

____

If evidence of thought insertion, **Were these thoughts/images/impulses ever imposed by something outside of you?**

YES ____ NO ____

If YES, specify ____

4. **In what way did these thoughts/images/impulses concern you?; What did you worry that having these thoughts/images/impulses might mean?**

____

____

B. Compulsions

If no evidence of compulsions has been obtained, skip to Past Episode (Obsessions & Compulsions; p. 39).

Now I want to ask you a series of questions about the past period or repetitive behaviors or mental actions that began roughly in ________ and ended roughly in ________ (specify month/year).

List principal compulsions: 1: ____

2: ____

Inquire for each compulsion:

1a. **On the average day during that period, what percentage of the day were you ______________?**

#1: ________ % #2: ________ % Overall: ________ %

b. If uncertain, **Did you typically spend at least an hour a day performing these behaviors/mental actions?**

YES ____ NO ____

2. **Did you feel that repeating these behaviors/mental actions didn't make sense or took up more time than was really necessary?**

YES ____ NO ____

Specify: ____________________

If NO, At any time during that past period when you were bothered by these behaviors/mental acts, did you feel that they didn't make sense or took up more time than necessary?

YES ____ NO ____

Specify: ____________________

3a. **How often did you resist carrying out these behaviors/mental acts?**

____

b. **How anxious did you feel if you couldn't or didn't carry out these acts?**

____

c. **What did you worry might happen if you didn't carry out these acts?**

____

C. Past Episode (Obsessions and/or Compulsions)

1. **In what ways did these repetitive thoughts/images/impulses/behaviors interfere with your life (e.g., daily routine, job, social activities)?; How much were you bothered about having these symptoms?**

____

____

Rate interference: __________ distress: __________

0----------1----------2----------3---------4----------5----------6----------7----------8
None Mild Moderate Severe Very severe

2. **Over the entire past period of time when you were having these repetitive thoughts/images/impulses/behaviors, were you regularly taking any types of drugs** (include drugs of abuse, medication)?

YES ____ NO ____

Specify (type; amount; dates of use): ____________________

____

3. **During that past period of time when you were having the repetitive thoughts/images/impulses/behaviors, did you have any physical condition?**

YES ____ NO ____

Specify (type; date of onset/remission): ____________________

____

4a. **For that past period of time, when did these repetitive thoughts/images/impulses/behaviors become a problem in that they occurred persistently (over an hour per day), you were bothered by the symptoms, or they interfered with your life in some way?** (Note: if patient is vague in date of onset, attempt to ascertain more specific information, e.g., by linking onset to objective life events.)

____

Date of Onset: __________ Month __________ Year

b. **Can you recall anything that might have led to this problem?** ______________________

____

c. **Were you under any type of stress during this time?**

YES ____ NO ____

What was happening in your life at the time?

____

____

Were you experiencing any difficulties or changes in:

(1) **Family/relationships?** ______________________

(2) **Work/school?** ______________________

(3) **Finances?** ______________________

(4) **Legal matters?** ______________________

(5) **Health** (self/others)? ______________________

5a. **When were these symptoms no longer a problem, in that they no longer were time-consuming or occurred repeatedly, you were not bothered by the symptoms, and they did not interfere with your life?**

____

Date of Remission: __________ Month __________ Year

b. **Can you recall any reasons why these symptoms subsided?**

____

6. **(Prior to/after) this past period of repetitive thoughts/images/impulses/behaviors, have there been other, separate periods of time that we haven't covered when you have had the same problems?**

YES ____ NO ____

If YES, go back and ask 2b. and 2c. from INITIAL INQUIRY (p. 31).

If NO, skip to SPECIFIC PHOBIA (p. 41).

SPECIFIC PHOBIA

I. INITIAL INQUIRY

For each situation, make separate ratings for level of fear and degree of avoidance using the following scale:

0	1	2	3	4	5	6	7	8
No fear/ Never avoids		Mild fear/ Rarely avoids		Moderate fear/ Sometimes avoids		Severe fear/ Often avoids		Very severe fear/ Always avoids

For each situation, inquire for both current and past episodes:

1. **Currently, do you fear or feel a need to avoid such things as:**
   Have you ever feared or felt a need to avoid such things as:

If patient endorses a current specific fear, when inquiring about past fears of the same object/situation, this inquiry should be for the presence of prior discrete episodes of disturbance (e.g., "**Since the fear began, have there been periods of time when you were not bothered by it?**"). Use space for comments to record other clinically useful information (e.g., frequency with which feared situation arises).

	CURRENT FEAR	CURRENT AVOID	COMMENTS	PAST FEAR	PAST AVOID
a. Animals (e.g., snakes, spiders, dogs, bees/insects)	____	____	____________	____	____
b. Natural Environment					
Heights	____	____	____________	____	____
Storms	____	____	____________	____	____
Water	____	____	____________	____	____
c. Blood/injection/injury: self					
Blood from minor cut	____	____	____________	____	____
Receiving injections	____	____	____________	____	____
Having blood drawn	____	____	____________	____	____
d. Blood/injection/injury: others					
Blood from minor cut	____	____	____________	____	____
Receiving injections	____	____	____________	____	____
Having blood drawn	____	____	____________	____	____
e. Situational					
Air travel	____	____	____________	____	____
Elevators/small enclosed places	____	____	____________	____	____
Driving	____	____	____________	____	____
f. Other					
Dental/medical procedures	____	____	____________	____	____
Choking	____	____	____________	____	____
Vomiting	____	____	____________	____	____
Contracting an illness	____	____	____________	____	____

****

If no evidence is found for fear/avoidance,
Skip to **PTSD** (p. 47).

****

II. CURRENT EPISODES

Complete for each specific fear that is potentially of clinical severity:

If evidence of a discrete past episode, preface inquiry in this section with: **Now I want to ask you a series of questions about your current specific fears.**

A. Specific fear #1: ______________________________

1. **What are you concerned will happen in this situation?** ______________________________

____

2. **Do you experience the anxiety nearly every time you encounter** ______________________________?

YES ____ NO ____

3. **Does the anxiety occur as soon as you enter the situation or are about to enter the situation, or is the anxiety sometimes delayed or unexpected?**

IMMEDIATE ____ DELAYED ____

4a. **Are you anxious about this situation because you are afraid that you will have an unexpected panic attack?**

YES ____ NO ____

If YES,

b. **Other than times when you are exposed to ____________, have you experienced an unexpected rush of fear/anxiety?**

YES ____ NO ____

If YES, **where has this occurred?** ______________________________

If YES to 4a. or 4b., consider whether fear could be subsumed into panic disorder.

5. **In what ways has this fear interfered with your life (e.g., daily routine, job, social activities)?; How much are you bothered by this fear?**

____

____

Rate interference: ____________ distress: ____________

0----------1----------2----------3----------4----------5----------6----------7----------8

None Mild Moderate Severe Very severe

6a. **When did the anxiety about ____________ begin to be a problem in that it caused a lot of distress or interference with your life?** (Note: if patient is vague in date of onset, attempt to ascertain more specific information, e.g., by linking onset to objective life events.)

____

Date of Onset: ____________ Month ____________ Year

b. **Can you recall anything that might have led to this fear?** ______________________________

____

B. Specific fear #2: ____

1. **What are you concerned will happen in this situation?** ______________________________

____

2. **Do you experience the anxiety nearly every time you encounter** ______________________?

YES ____ NO ____

3. **Does the anxiety occur as soon as you enter the situation or are about to enter the situation, or is the anxiety sometimes delayed or unexpected?**

IMMEDIATE ____ DELAYED ____

4a. **Are you anxious about this situation because you are afraid that you will have an unexpected panic attack?**

YES ____ NO ____

If YES,

b. **Other than times when you are exposed to ___________, have you experienced an unexpected rush of fear/anxiety?**

YES ____ NO ____

If YES, where has this occurred? ______________________________

If YES to 4a. or 4b., consider whether fear could be subsumed into panic disorder.

5. **In what ways has this fear interfered with your life (e.g., daily routine, job, social activities)?; How much are you bothered by this fear?**

____

____

Rate interference: __________ distress: __________

0----------1----------2----------3----------4----------5----------6----------7----------8
None Mild Moderate Severe Very severe

6a. **When did the anxiety about _________ begin to be a problem in that it caused a lot of distress or interference with your life?** (Note: if patient is vague in date of onset, attempt to ascertain more specific information, e.g., by linking onset to objective life events.)

____

Date of Onset: __________ Month __________ Year

b. **Can you recall anything that might have led to this fear?** ______________________

____

III. PAST EPISODES

Complete for each specific fear that was potentially of clinical severity:

Now I want to ask you a series of questions about your <u>past</u> specific fears:

A. Specific fear #1: ______________________________

1. **What were you concerned would happen in this situation?** ______________________________

____

2. **Did you experience the anxiety nearly every time you encountered** ______________?

YES ____ NO ____

3. **Did the anxiety occur as soon as you entered the situation or were about to enter the situation, or was the anxiety sometimes delayed or unexpected?**

IMMEDIATE ____ DELAYED ____

4a. **Were you anxious about this situation because you were afraid that you would have an unexpected panic attack?**

YES ____ NO ____

If YES,

b. **Other than times when you were exposed to __________, had you experienced an unexpected rush of fear/anxiety?**

YES ____ NO ____

If YES, **where did that occur?** ______________________________

If YES to 4a. or 4b., consider whether fear could be subsumed into panic disorder.

5. **In what ways did this fear interfere with your life (e.g., daily routine, job, social activities)?; How much were you bothered by this fear?**

____

____

Rate interference: __________ distress: __________

0----------1----------2----------3----------4----------5----------6----------7----------8
None Mild Moderate Severe Very severe

6a. **When did the anxiety about __________ begin to be a problem in that it caused a lot of distress or interference with your life?** (Note: if patient is vague in date of onset, attempt to ascertain more specific information, e.g., by linking onset to objective life events.)

____

Date of Onset: __________ Month __________ Year

b. **Can you recall anything that might have led to this fear?** ______________________________

____

7a. **When was the anxiety about _________ no longer a problem in that you were comfortable with __________, or it no longer caused a lot of distress or interference with your life?**

____

Date of Remission: ___________ Month ____________ Year

b. **Can you recall any reasons why you were no longer anxious about this situation?**

____

B. Specific fear #2: ____

1. **What were you concerned would happen in this situation?** _______________________________

____

2. **Did you experience the anxiety nearly every time you encountered _______________________?**

YES ____ NO ____

3. **Did the anxiety occur as soon as you entered the situation or were about to enter the situation, or was the anxiety sometimes delayed or unexpected?**

IMMEDIATE ____ DELAYED ____

4a. **Were you anxious about this situation because you were afraid that you would have an unexpected panic attack?**

YES ____ NO ____

If YES,

b. **Other than times when you were exposed to ____________, had you experienced an unexpected rush of fear/anxiety?**

YES ____ NO ____

If YES, **where did that occur?** ____

If YES to 4a. or 4b., consider whether fear could be subsumed into panic disorder.

5. **In what ways did this fear interfere with your life (e.g., daily routine, job, social activities)?; How much were you bothered by this fear?**

____

____

Rate interference: ___________ distress: ___________

0----------1----------2----------3----------4----------5----------6----------7----------8

None Mild Moderate Severe Very severe

6a. **When did the anxiety about __________ begin to be a problem in that it caused a lot of distress or interference with your life?** (Note: if patient is vague in date of onset, attempt to ascertain more specific information, e.g., by linking onset to objective life events.)

____

Date of Onset: ___________ Month ____________ Year

b. **Can you recall anything that might have led to this fear?** ______________________________

____

7a. **When was the anxiety about ________ no longer a problem in that you were comfortable with ________, or it no longer caused a lot of distress or interference with your life?**

____

Date of Remission: __________ Month __________ Year

b. **Can you recall any reasons why you were no longer anxious about this situation?** __________

____

IV. RESEARCH

Inquiry should pertain to current episodes of disturbance.

A. PANIC ATTACK SYMPTOMS

1. Specific fear #1: ____

Do you experience ____________ when you encounter __________?

0----------1----------2----------3----------4----------5----------6----------7----------8
None Mild Moderate Severe Very severe

1. Palpitations, pounding heart, or accelerated heart rate ___
2. Sweating ___
3. Trembling or shaking ___
4. Shortness of breath or smothering sensations ___
5. Feeling of choking ___
6. Chest pain or discomfort ___
7. Nausea or stomach distress ___
8. Chills, hot flushes, or blushing ___
9. Dizziness, unsteady feelings, lightheadedness, or faintness ___
10. Feelings of unreality or being detached from oneself ___
11. Numbing or tingling sensations ___
12. Fear of dying ___
13. Fear of going crazy ___
14. Fear of doing something uncontrolled ___

1. Specific fear #2: ____

Do you experience ____________ when you encounter __________?

0----------1----------2----------3----------4----------5----------6----------7----------8
None Mild Moderate Severe Very severe

1. Palpitations, pounding heart, or accelerated heart rate ___
2. Sweating ___
3. Trembling or shaking ___
4. Shortness of breath or smothering sensations ___
5. Feeling of choking ___
6. Chest pain or discomfort ___
7. Nausea or stomach distress ___
8. Chills, hot flushes, or blushing ___
9. Dizziness, unsteady feelings, lightheadedness, or faintness ___
10. Feelings of unreality or being detached from oneself ___
11. Numbing or tingling sensations ___
12. Fear of dying ___
13. Fear of going crazy ___
14. Fear of doing something uncontrolled ___

POSTTRAUMATIC STRESS DISORDER/ACUTE STRESS DISORDER

I. INITIAL INQUIRY

1a. **Have you ever experienced or witnessed a traumatic or life-threatening event such as assault, rape, seeing someone badly injured or killed, combat, accidents, or natural or man-made disasters?**

YES ____ NO ____

If YES, specify nature and date of event(s); specify date trauma ended if the event persisted (e.g., ongoing physical abuse):

____

____

b. **Do you recall any events of this nature occurring when you were a child?**

YES ____ NO ____

If YES, specify nature and date of event(s); specify date trauma ended if the event persisted (e.g., ongoing physical abuse):

____

____

****

If NO to both 1a. and 1b.,
Skip to **MAJOR DEPRESSION** (p. 55).

****

c. **What was your emotional response while the event was occurring?** (Specify for each trauma reported in 1a. and 1b.)

____

____

If uncertain, **While the event was occurring, did you experience intense fear, helplessness, or horror?**

YES ____ NO ____

d. **Currently, are you being bothered by such things as recurrent memories, thoughts, or dreams about the event, or distress when you hear or see things that remind you of the event?**

YES ____ NO ____

If YES, **How soon after the event occurred/began did you begin having these symptoms?**

____

Skip to 2a.

e. If NO, **Since the event occurred, have you <u>ever</u> been bothered by such things as recurrent and distressing memories, dreams, or thoughts about the event?**

YES ____ NO ____

If NO, skip to 3.

After the event occurred, how soon did you begin to experience these distressing thoughts/memories/dreams?; When did these symptoms stop?

____

____

2a. **Besides this current/most recent time when you have been experiencing these recurrent and distressing memories/thoughts/dreams of the event, have there been other, separate periods of time when you have experienced similar symptoms?**

YES ____ NO ____

If NO, skip to 3.

b. **So prior to this current/most recent period of time when you been experiencing these recurrent and distressing memories/thoughts/dreams of the event, there was a considerable period of time when you were not having these symptoms?**

YES ____ NO ____

c. **How much time separated these periods?; When did this/these separate period(s) occur?**

____

3. Re-experiencing Symptoms

If patient does not report current or past re-experiencing symptoms (i.e., NO to 1d. and 1e.), inquire about PAST only (using queries below keyed to the month after the trauma occurred/began). If patient reports current or past re-experiencing symptoms, (i.e., YES to either 1d. or 1e.), inquire about both CURRENT and PAST symptoms. Particularly if there is evidence of <u>separate</u> episodes, inquire for the presence of prior <u>discrete</u> episodes of disturbance (e.g., **"Since these symptoms began, have there been periods of time when you were not bothered by them?"**). Use the space below each symptom to record the specific nature of that symptom (e.g., cues that elicit distress associated with the trauma). Use comment section to record clinically useful information (e.g., data pertaining to the discreteness of episodes, duration of symptom more consistent with Acute Stress Disorder).

For each re-experiencing symptom, make ratings of Recurrence/Distress (i.e., frequency and intensity) using the scale and suggested queries below.

RECURRENCE/DISTRESS:

Inquiry for patients who respond YES to either items 1d. or 1e.:

How often do/did you experience ________?; How much distress does/did this produce?

Inquiry for patients who respond NO to Items 1d. and 1e.:

Within a month after the event occurred/began, did you experience ________?; How often do/did you experience ________?; How much distress does/did this produce?

0----------1----------2----------3----------4----------5----------6----------7----------8

0	2	4	6	8
No/ No distress	Rarely/ Mild distress	Occasionally/ Moderate distress	Frequently/ Severe distress	Constantly/ Extreme distress

	CURRENT	COMMENTS	PAST
a. Intrusive recollections of the event (including images, thoughts, perceptions) ______	____	______	____
b. Dreams of the event ______	____	______	____
c. Acting or feeling as if the event were recurring (e.g., flashbacks, hallucinations, illusions, reliving the trauma) ______	____	______	____
d. Emotional distress at exposure to internal or external cues that are reminders of the event ______	____	______	____
e. Physical response at exposure to internal or external cues that are reminders of the event ______	____	______	____

****

If no evidence of current or past re-experiencing symptoms,
Skip to **MAJOR DEPRESSION** (p. 55).

****

II. CURRENT EPISODE

If evidence of a discrete past episode, preface inquiry in this section with: **Now I want to ask you a series of questions about this <u>current</u> period when you have been experiencing recurrent and distressing memories/dreams/thoughts of the event, beginning roughly in** _________ (specify month/year).

Specify traumatic event: ______________________________

1. **Since the event occurred/began, how often have you experienced__________?; To what degree have you experienced __________?; Have you had this symptom only since the event occurred/began?** (Do not record symptoms that are associated with other conditions such as panic, depression, generalized anxiety, etc.)

0----------1----------2----------3----------4----------5----------6----------7----------8

0	2	4	6	8
Never/ None	Rarely/ Mild	Occasionally/ Moderate	Frequently/ Severe	Constantly/ Very severe

	SEVERITY	ONSET SINCE TRAUMA
a. avoidance of thoughts, feelings, or conversations associated with event	____	----
b. avoidance of activities, situations, or people that are reminders of the event	____	----
c. inability to recall important aspect of the event	____	----
d. loss of interest and/or decreased participation in significant activities	____	Y N
e. feeling detached or emotionally distant from others	____	Y N

	SEVERITY	ONSET SINCE TRAUMA
f. restricted emotions (e.g., unable to have pleasant or loving feelings)	____	Y N
g. sense of foreshortened future (e.g., does not expect career, marriage, normal life span)	____	Y N

2. **Since the event occurred/began, how often have you experienced__________?; To what degree have you experienced __________?; Have you had this symptom only since the event occurred/began?** (Do not record symptoms that are associated with other conditions such as panic, depression, generalized anxiety, etc.)

0----------1----------2----------3----------4----------5----------6----------7----------8

Never/ None	Rarely/ Mild	Occasionally/ Moderate	Frequently/ Severe	Constantly/ Very severe

	SEVERITY	ONSET SINCE TRAUMA
a. difficulty falling or staying asleep	____	Y N
b. irritability or outbursts of anger	____	Y N
c. difficulty concentrating	____	Y N
d. hypervigilance (e.g., constant vigilance of surroundings)	____	Y N
e. exaggerated startle response	____	Y N

3. **In what ways have these recurrent and distressing memories/thoughts/dreams and the symptoms associated with them interfered with your life (e.g., daily routine, job, social activities)?; How much are you bothered by these symptoms?**

____

____

Rate interference: __________ distress: __________

0----------1----------2----------3----------4----------5----------6----------7----------8

Never/ None	Rarely/ Mild	Occasionally/ Moderate	Frequently/ Severe	Constantly/ Very severe

If there is any uncertainty regarding when the traumatic event occurred/began, ask:

4a. **Do you recall the specific date that the event occurred/began?** (Note: if patient is vague in date of occurrence, attempt to ascertain more specific information, e.g., by linking onset to objective life events.)

____

Date of Event: __________ Month __________ Year

For events that were ongoing (e.g., recurrent physical abuse), ask:

b. **Do you recall the specific date that the event ended?**

____

Date Event Ended: __________ Month __________ Year

If there is any uncertainty regarding the onset of the disorder, ask:

5a. **For this current period of time, when did these recurrent and distressing memories/thoughts/ dreams and the symptoms associated with them become a problem in that they occurred persistently, you were bothered by the symptoms and they interfered with your life in some way?** (Note: if patient is vague in date of onset, attempt to ascertain more specific information, e.g., by linking onset to objective life events.)

____

Date of Onset: __________ Month __________ Year

b. **How soon after the event occurred/began did you begin having the recurrent and distressing memories/thoughts/dreams as well as the other symptoms associated with them?**

____

Note: Assign PTSD with Delayed Onset if syndrome began at least 6 months after the stressor. If symptoms occurred within four weeks of the event and lasted no longer than four weeks, consider Acute Stress Disorder (p. 54).

6. **Besides this current period of time when you've been having these recurrent and distressing memories/thoughts/dreams, have there been other, separate periods of time before this when you have had the same problems either in relation to this event or to another event?**

YES ____ NO ____

If YES, go back and ask 2b. and 2c. from INITIAL INQUIRY (p. 47). If there is evidence of an additional traumatic event, record the nature and dates of this event in 1a. or 1b.

If NO, skip to MAJOR DEPRESSION (p. 55).

III. PAST EPISODE

Now I want to ask you a series of questions about the past period when you had been experiencing recurrent and distressing memories/dreams/thoughts of the event that began roughly in _______ and ended roughly in _________ (specify months/years).

Specify traumatic event: ____

1. **After the event occurred/began, how often did you experience __________?; To what degree did you experience __________?; Did you have this symptom only after the event occurred/began?** (Do not record symptoms that are associated with other conditions such as panic, depression, generalized anxiety, etc.)

0----------1----------2----------3----------4----------5----------6----------7----------8

0	2	4	6	8
Never/ None	Rarely/ Mild	Occasionally/ Moderate	Frequently/ Severe	Constantly/ Very severe

	SEVERITY	ONSET SINCE TRAUMA
a. avoidance of thoughts, feelings, or conversations associated with event	____	----
b. avoidance of activities, situations, or people that are reminders of the event	____	----
c. inability to recall important aspect of the event	____	----
d. loss of interest and/or decreased participation in significant activities	____	Y N
e. feeling detached or emotionally distant from others	____	Y N

0----------1----------2----------3----------4----------5----------6----------7----------8

Never/ None	Rarely/ Mild	Occasionally/ Moderate	Frequently/ Severe	Constantly/ Very severe

	SEVERITY	ONSET SINCE TRAUMA
f. restricted emotions (e.g., unable to have pleasant or loving feelings)	____	Y N
g. sense of foreshortened future (e.g., does not expect career, marriage, normal lifespan)	____	Y N

2. **After the event occurred/began, how often did you experience __________?; To what degree did you experience __________?; Did you have this symptom only after the event occurred/began?** (Do not record symptoms that are associated with other conditions such as panic, depression, generalized anxiety, etc.)

0----------1----------2----------3----------4----------5----------6----------7----------8

Never/ None	Rarely/ Mild	Occasionally/ Moderate	Frequently/ Severe	Constantly/ Very severe

	SEVERITY	ONSET SINCE TRAUMA
a. difficulty falling or staying asleep	____	Y N
b. irritability or outbursts of anger	____	Y N
c. difficulty concentrating	____	Y N
d. hypervigilance (e.g., constant vigilance of surroundings)	____	Y N
e. exaggerated startle response	____	Y N

3. **In what ways did these recurrent and distressing memories/thoughts/dreams and the symptoms associated with them interfere with your life (e.g., daily routine, job, social activities)?; How much were you bothered by these symptoms?**

____

____

Rate interference: __________ distress: __________

0----------1----------2----------3----------4----------5----------6----------7----------8

None	Mild	Moderate	Severe	Very Severe

If there is any uncertainty regarding when the traumatic event occurred/began, ask:

4a. **Do you recall the specific date that the event occurred/began?** (Note: if patient is vague in date of occurrence, attempt to ascertain more specific information, e.g., by linking onset to objective life events.)

____

Date of Event: __________ Month __________ Year

For events that were ongoing (e.g., recurrent physical abuse), ask:

b. **Do you recall the specific date that the event ended?**

____

Date Event Ended: __________ Month __________ Year

If there is any uncertainty regarding the onset of the disorder, ask:

5a. **For that past period of time, when did these recurrent and distressing memories/thoughts/dreams and the symptoms associated with them become a problem in that they occurred persistently, you were bothered by the symptoms and they interfered with your life in some way?** (Note: if patient is vague in date of onset, attempt to ascertain more specific information, e.g., by linking onset to objective life events.)

____

Date of Onset: __________ Month __________ Year

b. **How soon after the event occurred/began did you begin having the recurrent and distressing memories/thoughts/dreams as well as the other symptoms associated with them?**

____

Note: Assign PTSD with Delayed Onset if syndrome began at least 6 months after the stressor. If symptoms occurred within four weeks of the event and lasted no longer than four weeks, consider Acute Stress Disorder (p. 54).

6a. **When was this no longer a problem, in that the memories/thoughts/dreams did not occur persistently, you weren't bothered by them, and these memories and the symptoms associated with them did not interfere with your life?**

Date of Remission: __________ Month __________ Year

b. **Can you recall any reasons why these symptoms were no longer a problem for you?**

____

____

7. **Prior to/after this past period of recurrent and distressing memories/thoughts/dreams, have there been other, separate periods of time that we haven't covered when you have had the same problems either in relation to this event or to another event?**

YES ____ NO ____

If YES, go back and ask 2b. and 2c. from INITIAL INQUIRY (p. 47). If there is evidence of an additional traumatic event, record the nature and dates of this event in 1a. or 1b.

IF NO, skip to MAJOR DEPRESSION (p. 55).

IV. ACUTE DISTRESS DISORDER

If it has been determined that the patient has experienced a traumatic event associated with symptoms of re-experiencing and avoidance of trauma-related stimuli and symptoms of marked arousal/anxiety that emerged within four weeks of the event and lasted no longer than four weeks, administer this section.

Specify traumatic event: ______________________________

1. **After the event occurred/began, how often do/did you experience __________?; To what degree do/did you experience __________?** (Do not record symptoms that are associated with other conditions such as panic, depression, generalized anxiety, etc.)

0----------1----------2----------3----------4----------5----------6----------7----------8

0	2	4	6	8
Never/ None	Rarely/ Mild	Occasionally/ Moderate	Frequently/ Severe	Constantly/ Very severe

	SEVERITY		
	CURRENT	COMMENTS	PAST
a. sense of numbing, detachment, or absence of emotional responsiveness	___	___	___
b. decreased awareness of surroundings (e.g., being in a "daze")	___	___	___
c. derealization	___	___	___
d. depersonalization	___	___	___
e. inability to recall an important aspect of the event	___	___	___
f. being restless, unable to sit still	___	___	___

Note: Rating for motor restlessness (1f.) applies not to the B criterion of Acute Stress Disorder but to the E criterion (the remaining symptoms of the E criterion are rated previously in PTSD).

2a. **How long after the event occurred/began, did you begin to experience these symptoms?**

CURRENT: ______________________________

PAST: ______________________________

If inquiring about a PAST disorder ask:

b. **How long did these symptoms last?**

____

3. **During this period when you were/have been having these symptoms, (were you/have you been) regularly taking any types of drugs?** (Include drugs of abuse, medication.)

YES ___ NO ___

Specify (type; amount; dates of use):

CURRENT: ______________________________

PAST: ______________________________

4. **During this/that period, did/do you have any physical conditions?**

YES ___ NO ___

Specify (type; date of onset/remission):

CURRENT: ______________________________

PAST: ______________________________

MAJOR DEPRESSIVE EPISODE

I. INITIAL INQUIRY

1a. **Currently, have you been feeling depressed, sad, empty, or have you lost interest or pleasure in almost all of your usual activities?**

Depressed:	YES ___	NO ___
Loss of interest:	YES ___	NO ___

b. **Currently, have other people commented to you that you appear down or tearful or that you seem less interested in your usual activities?**

Depressed:	YES ___	NO ___
Loss of interest:	YES ___	NO ___

If NO to 1a. and 1b., continue to 1c.

If YES to either 1a. or 1b., skip to 2a.

c. **Have you ever experienced a period of two weeks or more when you felt depressed, sad, empty, or lost interest or pleasure in your usual activities?**

Depressed:	YES ___	NO ___
Loss of interest:	YES ___	NO ___

If YES, **When was the most recent time this occurred?**

____

****

If YES to either 1a., 1b., 1c., or uncertain, continue inquiry.
Otherwise skip to **DYSTHYMIC DISORDER** (p. 61).

****

2a. **Besides this current/most recent period of time when you have felt depressed or lost interest in your usual activities, have there been other, separate periods of time when you felt this way?**

YES ___ NO ___

If NO, skip to CURRENT EPISODE.

b. **So prior to this current/most recent period of time when you felt depressed or a loss of interest in your activities, there was a considerable period of time when you did not feel this way?**

YES ___ NO ___

c. **How much time separated these periods?; When did this/these separate period(s) occur?** (Determine if episodes were separated by an interval of at least 2 months without significant symptoms of depression.)

____

____

II. CURRENT EPISODE

If evidence of a discrete past episode, preface inquiry in this section with: **Now I want to ask you a series of questions about this current period of time when you felt [depressed/loss of interest] that began roughly in __________** (specify month/year).

1. **Have you been experiencing the feelings of [depression/loss of interest in usual activities] nearly every day over the past two weeks?**

Depressed:	YES ____	NO ____
Loss of interest:	YES ____	NO ____

2. **Over the past 2 weeks, have you experienced __________?; Have you experienced __________ nearly every day over the past 2 weeks?**

   (Record symptoms that have been present during the same two-week period and represent a change from previous functioning.)

0----------1----------2----------3----------4----------5----------6----------7----------8
None Mild Moderate Severe Very severe

	SEVERITY	NEARLY EVERY DAY
a. significant weight loss or weight gain (e.g., 5% of body weight within a month); decrease or increase in appetite	____	Y N
b. insomnia or hypersomnia	____	Y N
c. Psychomotor agitation or retardation **Unable to sit still or so slowed down that you can hardly move or carry on a conversation?** (must be observable)	____	Y N
d. Loss of energy or fatigue	____	Y N
e. Worthlessness or excessive, inappropriate guilt. **Do you blame yourself for anything or feel guilty?**	____	Y N
f. Impaired concentration, slowed thinking, or indecisiveness. **Thinking been slowed down, hard to make decisions?**	____	Y N
g. Recurrent thoughts of death or suicide **Think about death or hurting yourself? How much do you think about it?**	____	----

If YES to 2g., inquire about the extent of suicidal ideation or intent (e.g., history of prior attempts, presence/extent of current plan, access to method for carrying out plan, ability to state reasons for living):

____

____

3. **In what ways have these symptoms of depression interfered with your life (e.g., daily routine, job, social activities)?; How much are you bothered about having these symptoms?**

____

____

Rate interference: __________ distress: __________

0----------1----------2----------3----------4----------5----------6----------7----------8
None Mild Moderate Severe Very severe

4. **Over this entire current period of time when you've been experiencing these feelings, have you been regularly taking any types of drugs** (include drugs of abuse, medication)?

YES ____ NO ____

Specify (type; amount; dates of use): ______________________________

____

5. **During this current period of time when you've been having these feelings, have you had any physical condition** (e.g., pregnancy, hypothyroidism, hypoglycemia)?

YES ____ NO ____

Specify (type; date of onset/remission): ______________________________

____

6a. **For this current period of time, when did the depression and the symptoms accompanying the depression become a problem in that they occurred persistently (i.e., occurred nearly every day), you were bothered by these symptoms, or they interfered with your life in some way?** (Note: if patient is vague in date of onset, attempt to ascertain more specific information, e.g., by linking onset to objective life events.)

____

Date of Onset: ____________ Month ____________ Year

b. **Can you recall anything that might have led to this problem?**

____

____

c. **Were you under any type of stress during this time?**

YES ____ NO ____

What was happening in your life at the time?

____

____

Were you experiencing any difficulties or changes in:

(1) **Loss of a loved one?** ______________________________

(2) **Family/relationships?** ______________________________

(3) **Work/school?** ______________________________

(4) **Finances?** ______________________________

(5) **Legal matters?** ______________________________

(6) **Health** (self/others)? ______________________________

Note: If symptoms of depression occur within 2 months of the loss of a loved one, consider the diagnosis of Bereavement.

7. **Besides this current period of depression and/or loss of interest in usual activities, have there been other, separate periods of time before this when you have had the same problems?**

YES ____ NO ____

If YES, go back and ask 2b. and 2c. from INITIAL INQUIRY (p. 55).

If NO, skip to DYSTHYMIC DISORDER (p. 61).

III. PAST EPISODE

Now I want to ask you a series of questions about the past period(s) of [depression/loss of interest] that began roughly in _____ and ended roughly in _______ (specify months/years).

If there is evidence of more than one prior episode, ask:

What would you identify as the period of time when you experienced the feelings of [depression/loss of interest in usual activities] at their worst or most severe levels?

List dates (onset/remission) corresponding to periods of inquiry (if a current episode is reported as the worst episode, do not list below):

Worst/Past Episode #1: FROM ____________ TO ____________
Past Episode #2: FROM ____________ TO ____________

If a past episode is reported as the worst episode, inquire about this episode first:

1. **During that period of time in ________ (years), did you experience the feelings of [depression/loss of interest in usual activities] nearly every day for at least two weeks?**

Worst/Past Episode #1: YES ___ NO ___
Past Episode #2: YES ___ NO ___

2. **During that period of time in ________ (years), did you experience __________ ?; Did you experience _________ nearly every day for a period of 2 weeks or more?** (Record symptoms that were present during the same two-week period and represented a change from previous functioning.)

0----------1----------2----------3----------4----------5----------6----------7----------8
None Mild Moderate Severe Very severe

	Worst/Past Episode 1 SEV	Worst/Past Episode 1 Nearly Every Day	Past Episode 2 SEV	Past Episode 2 Nearly Every Day
a. significant weight loss or weight gain (e.g., 5% of body weight within a month); decrease or increase in appetite	____	Y N	____	Y N
b. insomnia or hypersomnia	____	Y N	____	Y N
c. Psychomotor agitation or retardation **Unable to sit still or so slowed down that you can hardly move or carry on a conversation?** (must be observable)	____	Y N	____	Y N
d. Loss of energy or fatigue	____	Y N	____	Y N
e. Worthlessness or excessive, inappropriate guilt. **Do you blame yourself for anything or feel guilty?**	____	Y N	____	Y N

	Worst/Past Episode 1 SEV	Worst/Past Episode 1 Nearly Every Day	Past Episode 2 SEV	Past Episode 2 Nearly Every Day
f. Impaired concentration, slowed thinking, or indecisiveness. **Thinking been slowed down, hard to make decisions?**	____	Y N	____	Y N
g. Recurrent thoughts of death or suicide **Think about death or hurting yourself? How much do you think about it?**	____	--	____	--

If YES to 2g., inquire about the extent of suicidal ideation or intent (e.g., suicide attempts, presence/extent of plan):

____

____

3. **In what ways did the symptoms of depression interfere with your life (e.g., daily routine, job, social activities)?; How much were you bothered about having these symptoms?**

____

____

#1: Rate interference: __________ distress: __________
#2: Rate interference: __________ distress: __________

0----------1----------2----------3----------4----------5----------6----------7----------8
None Mild Moderate Severe Very severe

4. **Over the entire period of time in** ______ (years) **when you were experiencing these feelings, were you regularly taking any types of drugs?** (Include drugs of abuse, medication.)

#1: YES ____ NO ____
#2: YES ____ NO ____

Specify (type; amount; dates of use): ____

____

5. **During the period of time in** ______ (years) **when you were having these feelings, did you have any physical condition** (e.g., pregnancy, hypothyroidism, hypoglycemia?)

#1: YES ____ NO ____
#2: YES ____ NO ____

Specify (type; date of onset/remission): ____

____

6a. **During the period of time in** ______ (years), **when did the depression and the symptoms accompanying the depression become a problem in that they occurred persistently (i.e., occurred nearly every day), you were bothered by these symptoms, or they interfered with your life in some way?** (Note: if patient is vague in date of onset, attempt to ascertain more specific information, e.g., by linking onset to objective life events.)

____

Date of Onset: __________ Month __________ Year

b. **Can you recall anything that might have led to this problem?**

#1: ____________________

#2: ____________________

c. **Were you under any type of stress during this time?**

#1: YES ____ NO ____
#2: YES ____ NO ____

What was happening in your life at the time?

#1: ____________________

#2: ____________________

Were you experiencing any difficulties or changes in:

(1) **Loss of a loved one?** #1: ____________________

#2: ____________________

(2) **Family/relationships?** #1: ____________________

#2: ____________________

(3) **Work/school?** #1: ____________________

#2: ____________________

(4) **Finances?** #1: ____________________

#2: ____________________

(5) **Legal matters?** #1: ____________________

#2: ____________________

(6) **Health** (self/others)? #1: ____________________

#2: ____________________

Note: If symptoms of depression occurred and remitted within 2 months of the loss of a loved one, consider the diagnosis of Bereavement.

7a. **When was the depression and symptoms accompanying the depression no longer a problem, in that they no longer occurred persistently, you were not bothered by these symptoms, and they did not interfere with your life?**

Date of Remission: #1: ________ Month ________ Year
#2: ________ Month ________ Year

b. **Can you recall any reasons why these feelings of depression subsided?**

#1: ____________________

#2: ____________________

8. **Prior to/after this past period of depression and/or loss of interest in usual activities, have there been other, separate periods of time that we haven't covered when you have had the same problems?**

YES ____ NO ____

If YES, go back and ask 2b. and 2c. from INITIAL INQUIRY (p. 55).

If NO, skip to DYSTHYMIC DISORDER (p. 61).

DYSTHYMIC DISORDER

I. INITIAL INQUIRY

If patient has met criteria for MAJOR DEPRESSION, preface the items in INITIAL INQUIRY with **"Other than during _______** (specify timeframe of MDE)"

1a. **Over the past 2 years, have you frequently had days where you felt down, blue, or depressed for most of the day?**

YES ____ NO ____

b. **Over the past 2 years, have other people commented to you that you often appear down, blue, or depressed?**

YES ____ NO ____

If NO to 1a. and 1b., continue to 1c.

If YES to either 1a. or 1b., skip to 2a.

c. **Have you ever experienced a period when you felt down, blue, or depressed, more days than not for 2 years or more?**

YES ____ NO ____

If YES, **When was the most recent time this occurred?**

____

****

If YES to either 1a., 1b., 1c., or uncertain, continue inquiry.
Otherwise skip to **MANIA/CYCLOTHYMIA** (p. 66).

****

2a. **Besides this current/most recent period of time when you have persistently felt down or depressed, have there been other, separate periods of 2 years or more when you felt this way?**

YES ____ NO ____

If NO, skip to CURRENT EPISODE.

b. **So prior to this current/most recent period of time when you felt down or depressed, there was a considerable period of time when you did not feel this way?**

YES ____ NO ____

c. **How much time separated these periods?; When did this/these separate period(s) occur?** [If a prior MDE exists, determine if the onset of dysthymia occurred after a full remission of the MDE (i.e., 6 months of no significant signs or symptoms of depression) or preceded the MDE by at least 2 years.]

____

____

II. CURRENT EPISODE

If evidence of a discrete past episode, preface inquiry in this section with: **Now I want to ask you a series of questions about this <u>current</u> period of time when you felt down or depressed that began roughly in** __________ (specify month/year).

1. **What percentage of the days over the past 2 years have you experienced a depressed mood for most of the day?**

   ________%

   If uncertain, **Have you felt this way more days than not over the past 2 years?**

   YES ____ NO ____

2. **Over the past 2 years, have you had periods of 2 months or more when your mood was normal?**

   YES ____ NO ____

   If YES, **When?** FROM ________ TO __________

3. **Over the past 2 years, have you often experienced** __________ **while depressed?; Over the past 2 years, has** _________ **occurred persistently without a period of 2 months or more when this symptom was not present?**

   0----------1----------2----------3----------4----------5----------6----------7----------8
   None — Mild — Moderate — Severe — Very severe

	SEVERITY	PERSISTENT
a. poor appetite or overeating	____	Y N
b. insomnia or hypersomnia. **Have trouble sleeping, or sleeping too much?**	____	Y N
c. low energy or fatigue. **Tired all the time?**	____	Y N
d. low self-esteem. **Down on yourself, feeling like a failure?**	____	Y N
e. poor concentration or difficulty making decisions	____	Y N
f. feelings of hopelessness. **Feeling pessimistic about the future?**	____	Y N

4. **In what ways have these symptoms of depression interfered with your life (e.g., daily routine, job, social activities)?; How much are you bothered about having these symptoms?**

   ____

   ____

   Rate interference: ___________ distress: ___________

   0----------1----------2----------3----------4----------5----------6----------7----------8
   None — Mild — Moderate — Severe — Very severe

5. **Over this entire current period of time when you've been experiencing these feelings, have you been regularly taking any types of drugs?** (Include drugs of abuse, medication.)

   YES ____ NO ____

   Specify (type; amount; dates of use): ______________________________________

   ____

6. **During this current period of time when you've been having these feelings, have you had any physical condition** (e.g., pregnancy, hypothyroidism, hypoglycemia)**?**

YES ____ NO ____

Specify (type; date of onset/remission): ______________________________

____

7a. **For this current period of time, when did the depression and the symptoms accompanying the depression become a problem in that they occurred persistently (i.e., occurred nearly every day), you were bothered by these symptoms, or they interfered with your life in some way?** (Note: if patient is vague in date of onset, attempt to ascertain more specific information, e.g., by linking onset to objective life events.)

____

Date of Onset: __________ Month __________ Year

b. **Can you recall anything that might have led to this problem?** ______________________________

____

____

c. **Were you under any type of stress during this time?**

YES ____ NO ____

What was happening in your life at the time?

____

____

Were you experiencing any difficulties or changes in:

(1) **Loss of a loved one?** ______________________________

(2) **Family/relationships?** ______________________________

(3) **Work/school?** ______________________________

(4) **Finances?** ______________________________

(5) **Legal matters?** ______________________________

(6) **Health** (self/others)**?** ______________________________

8. **Besides this current period of time, have there been other, separate periods when you have felt down or depressed more days than not for a period of two years or more?**

YES ____ NO ____

If YES, go back and ask 2b. and 2c. from INITIAL INQUIRY (p. 61).

If NO, skip to MANIA/CYCLOTHYMIA (p. 66).

III. PAST EPISODE

Now I want to ask you a series of questions about the past period of depression that began roughly in _____ and ended roughly in _____ (specify months/years).

1. **During that period of time in _______ (years), on average, what percentage of the days did you experience a depressed mood for most of the day?**

   _______%

   If uncertain, **On average, did you feel this way more days than not during this period** (of 2 years or more)?

   YES ____ NO ____

2. **During that period, did you have periods of 2 months or more when your mood was normal?**

   YES ____ NO ____

   If YES, **When?** FROM _________ TO _________

3. **During that period of time in _______ (years), did you often experience _________ while depressed?; Did _________ occur persistently throughout this time without a period of 2 months or more when this symptom was not present?**

   0----------1----------2----------3----------4----------5----------6----------7----------8
   None Mild Moderate Severe Very severe

	SEVERITY	PERSISTENT
a. poor appetite or overeating	____	Y N
b. insomnia or hypersomnia. **Have trouble sleeping, or sleeping too much?**	____	Y N
c. low energy or fatigue. **Tired all the time?**	____	Y N
d. low self-esteem. **Down on yourself, feeling like a failure?**	____	Y N
e. poor concentration or difficulty making decisions	____	Y N
f. feelings of hopelessness. **Feeling pessimistic about the future?**	____	Y N

4. **In what ways did these symptoms of depression interfere with your life (e.g., daily routine, job, social activities)?; How much were you bothered about having these symptoms?**

   ____

   ____

   Rate interference: __________ distress: __________

   0----------1----------2----------3----------4----------5----------6----------7----------8
   None Mild Moderate Severe Very severe

5. **Over that entire period of time when you were experiencing these feelings, did you regularly take any types of drugs?** (Include drugs of abuse, medication.)

   YES ____ NO ____

   Specify (type; amount; dates of use): ____

   ____

6. **During that period of time, did you have any physical condition** (e.g., pregnancy, hypothyroidism, hypoglycemia)?

YES ____ NO ____

Specify (type; date of onset/remission): ______________________________

____

7a. **For that past period of time, when did the depression and the symptoms accompanying the depression become a problem in that they occurred persistently (i.e., occurred nearly every day), you were bothered by these symptoms, or they interfered with your life in some way?** (Note: if patient is vague in date of onset, attempt to ascertain more specific information, e.g., by linking onset to objective life events.)

____

Date of Onset: __________ Month __________ Year

b. **Can you recall anything that might have led to this problem?** ______________

____

____

c. **Were you under any type of stress during this time?**

YES ____ NO ____

What was happening in your life at the time?

____

____

Were you experiencing any difficulties or changes in:

(1) **Loss of a loved one?** ______________________________

(2) **Family/relationships?** ______________________________

(3) **Work/school?** ______________________________

(4) **Finances?** ______________________________

(5) **Legal matters?** ______________________________

(6) **Health** (self/others)? ______________________________

8a. **When was the depression and symptoms accompanying the depression no longer a problem, in that they no longer occurred persistently, you were not bothered by these symptoms, and they did not interfere with your life?**

Date of Remission: __________ Month __________ Year

b. **Can you recall any reasons why these feelings of depression subsided?**

____

____

9. **Prior to/after this past period of depression, have there been other, separate periods of time that we haven't covered when you have had the same problems?**

YES ____ NO ____

If YES, go back and ask 2b. and 2c. from INITIAL INQUIRY (p. 61).

If NO, skip to MANIA/CYCLOTHYMIA (p. 66).

MANIA/CYCLOTHYMIA

I. INITIAL INQUIRY

1a. **Have you ever experienced a period of several days or more when you felt unusually or excessively high or irritable? This is very different from being in a good mood or feeling the effects of a substance. What I mean is a period where your felt persistently or abnormally high or irritable, perhaps along with such things as a decreased need for sleep, racing thoughts and distractibility, and an unusual increase in the number of activities you got involved in.**

YES ____ NO ____

If YES, **When was the most recent time this occurred?**

____

How long did this period last? ______________________________

****

If YES to 1a. or uncertain, continue inquiry.
Otherwise skip to **HYPOCHONDRIASIS** (p. 71).

****

2a. **Besides this current/most recent period of time when you have felt unusually high or irritable, have there been other, separate periods of time when you felt this way?**

YES ____ NO ____

If NO, skip to CURRENT/MOST RECENT EPISODE.

b. **So prior to this current/most recent period of time when you felt unusually high or irritable, there was a considerable period of time when you did not feel this way?**

YES ____ NO ____

c. **How much time separated these periods?; When did this/these separate period(s) occur?** (Determine if episodes were separated by an interval of at least 2 months without significant symptoms of mania, hypomania, or a change in polarity.)

____

____

II. CURRENT/MOST RECENT EPISODE

If evidence of a discrete past episode, preface inquiry in this section with: **Now I want to ask you a series of questions about this current/most recent period of time when you felt [unusually high/irritable] that began roughly in** _________ (specify month/year).

1. **[Currently/during that period of time in** ______ (years)**], did you experience** __________**?; Did you experience** _________ **nearly every day during this time?** (Record symptoms that are persistent and clearly different from patient's usual nondepressed mood.)

0----------1----------2----------3----------4----------5----------6----------7----------8

None	Mild	Moderate	Severe	Very severe

	SEVERITY	NEARLY EVERY DAY
a. irritability	____	Y N
b. elevated or expansive mood	____	Y N
c. inflated self-esteem or grandiosity	____	Y N
d. decreased need for sleep (e.g., feels rested after 3 hours of sleep)	____	Y N
e. more talkative than usual or pressure to keep talking	____	Y N
f. flight of ideas or feeling that thoughts are racing	____	Y N
g. distractibility	____	Y N
h. increase in activity (e.g., social, work) or agitation/restlessness	____	Y N
i. involvement in pleasurable activities with a high potential for painful consequences (e.g., buying sprees, foolish investments, sexual indiscretions)	____	Y N
j. Delusions or hallucinations	____	--

Content: ____________________

2. **For the (current/most recent) episode, how long did you experience the elevated/irritable mood and these accompanying symptoms?**

____

If uncertain: **Did these symptoms occur persistently for a week or more?**

YES ____ NO ____

If less than one week, **For four days?**

YES ____ NO ____

3. **In what ways have/did these symptoms interfere with your life (e.g., daily routine, job, social activities)?; Did these symptoms impair your judgment or require you to be hospitalized/supervised to prevent you from harming yourself or others?**

____

____

Rate interference: ________ distress: ________

0----------1----------2----------3----------4----------5----------6----------7----------8
None Mild Moderate Severe Very severe

4. **Over the entire period of time when you were experiencing these feelings, were you regularly taking any types of drugs?** (Include drugs of abuse, medications.)

YES ____ NO ____

Specify (type; amount; dates of use): ____________________

____

5. **During the period of time when you were having these feelings, did you have any physical condition** (e.g., hyperthyroidism)?

YES ____ NO ____

Specify (type; date of onset/remission): ____________________

____

6a. **For the current/most recent time, when did these feelings and the symptoms accompanying them become a problem in that they occurred persistently (i.e., occurred nearly every day) and excessively, and they interfered with your life in some way?** (Note: if patient is vague in date of onset, attempt to ascertain more specific information, e.g., by linking onset to objective life events, episode of depression.)

____

Date of Onset: __________ Month __________ Year

b. **Can you recall anything that might have led to this problem?** (Ensure that symptoms were not precipitated by antidepressant treatment such as medication, ECT, light therapy.)

____

____

____

c. **Were these feelings immediately preceded or followed by a period of depression?** [Place (hypo)manic episode in temporal context with any current or past episodes of depression.]

YES ____ NO ____

If YES, specify: ____

7. **When did these feelings subside?; During the past two years, have you experienced a period of two months or more when you did not feel either unusually high/irritable or down/depressed?**

____

____

Note: Consider Cyclothymic Disorder in the presence of numerous hypomanic episodes and periods of depression (not meeting major depression) over the past two years or more in the absence of a period of at least two months when patient's mood was normal.

8. **Besides this most recent period of feeling unusually high/irritable, have there been other, separate periods of time before this when you have had the same problems?**

YES ____ NO ____

If YES, go back and ask 2b. and 2c. from INITIAL INQUIRY (p. 66).

If NO, skip to HYPOCHONDRIASIS (p. 71).

III. PAST EPISODE(S)

Now I want to ask you a series of questions about the past period(s) of elevated mood/irritability that began roughly in _____ and ended roughly in _____ (specify months/years).

1. **During that period of time in ______ (years), did you experience __________ ?; Did you experience __________ nearly every day during this time?** (Record symptoms that are persistent and clearly different from patient's usual nondepressed mood.)

0----------1----------2----------3----------4----------5----------6----------7----------8

None | Mild | Moderate | Severe | Very severe

	SEVERITY	NEARLY EVERY DAY
a. irritability	____	Y N
b. elevated or expansive mood	____	Y N
c. inflated self-esteem or grandiosity	____	Y N
d. decreased need for sleep (e.g., feels rested after 3 hours of sleep)	____	Y N
e. more talkative than usual or pressure to keep talking	____	Y N
f. flight of ideas or feeling that thoughts are racing	____	Y N
g. distractibility	____	Y N
h. increase in activity (e.g., social, work) or agitation/restlessness	____	Y N
i. involvement in pleasurable activities with a high potential for painful consequences (e.g., buying sprees, foolish investments, sexual indiscretions)	____	Y N
j. Delusions or hallucinations	____	--

Content: ____________________

2. **During that episode, how long did you experience the elevated/irritable mood and these accompanying symptoms?**

____

If uncertain: **Did these symptoms occur persistently for a week or more?**

YES ____ NO ____

If less than one week, **For four days?**

YES ____ NO ____

3. **In what ways did these symptoms interfere with your life (e.g., daily routine, job, social activities)?; Did these symptoms impair your judgment or require you to be hospitalized/supervised to prevent you from harming yourself or others?**

____

____

Rate interference: __________ distress: __________

0----------1----------2----------3----------4----------5----------6----------7----------8

None Mild Moderate Severe Very severe

4. **Over the entire period of time when you were experiencing these feelings, were you regularly taking any types of drugs?** (Include drugs of abuse, medications.)

YES ____ NO ____

Specify (type; amount; dates of use): ____________________

____

5. **During the period of time when you were having these feelings, did you have any physical condition** (e.g., hyperthyroidism)**?**

YES ____ NO ____

Specify (type; date of onset/remission): ____________________

____

6a. **During that episode, when did these feelings and the symptoms accompanying the them become a problem in that they occurred persistently (i.e., occurred nearly every day) and excessively, and they interfered with your life in some way?** (Note: if patient is vague in date of onset, attempt to ascertain more specific information, e.g., by linking onset to objective life events, episode of depression.)

____

Date of Onset: __________ Month __________ Year

b. **Can you recall anything that might have led to this problem?** (Ensure that symptoms were not precipitated by antidepressant treatment such as medication, ECT, light therapy.)

____

____

____

c. **Were these feelings immediately preceded or followed by a period of depression?** [Place (hypo)manic episode in temporal context with any current or past episodes of depression.]

YES ____ NO ____

If YES, specify: ______________________________

7. **When did these feelings subside?; During that period, did you experience a period of two months or more when you did not feel either unusually high/irritable or down/depressed?**

____

____

Note: Consider Cyclothymic Disorder in the presence of numerous hypomanic episodes and periods of depression (not meeting major depression) over two years or more in the absence of a period of at least two months when patient's mood was normal.

8. **Prior to/after this past period when you felt unusually high/irritable, have there been other, separate periods of time that we haven't covered when you have had the same problems?**

YES ____ NO ____

If YES, go back and ask 2b. and 2c. from INITIAL INQUIRY (p. 66).

If NO, skip to HYPOCHONDRIASIS (p. 71).

HYPOCHONDRIASIS

I. INITIAL INQUIRY

1a. **Over the last several months, have you continually feared or believed that you might have a serious physical disease or illness** (cancer, heart disease, AIDS, etc.)?

YES ____ NO ____

If NO, skip to 1b.

What types of diseases or illnesses do you fear you might have? ____________________

____

Skip to 2a.

b. **Have you ever experienced an extended period when you continually feared or believed that you might have had a serious physical disease or illness?**

YES ____ NO ____

If YES, **What types of diseases or illnesses did you fear you had?** ____________________

____

When was the most recent time this occurred?

____

****

If YES to either 1a. or 1b., or uncertain, continue inquiry.
Otherwise, skip to **SOMATIZATION DISORDER** (p. 76).

****

2a. **Besides this current/most recent period of time when you feared that you've had a serious disease or illness, have there been other, separate periods of time when you continually feared or believed that you had a serious physical disease or illness?**

YES ____ NO ____

If NO, skip to CURRENT EPISODE.

b. **So prior to this current/most recent period of time when you feared that you've had a serious disease or illness, there was a considerable period of time when you did not fear or believe that you had a serious physical disease or illness?**

YES ____ NO ____

c. **How much time separated these periods?; When did this/these separat period(s) occur?**

____

II. CURRENT EPISODE

If evidence of a discrete past episode, preface inquiry in this section with: **Now I want to ask you a series of questions about this current period of time when you feared or believed that you've had a serious disease or illness, that began roughly in** ________ (specify month/year).

List diseases/illnesses of inquiry: ____________________

1a. **Do you experience certain bodily symptoms or sensations that are associated with your fear or belief that you have** _________ (specify disease)?

YES ____ NO ____

If YES,

b. **What symptoms do you experience?**

____

c. **How often do these symptoms occur?**

____

2a. **Have you seen a doctor to determine whether you have _______ or any other physical illness?**

YES ____ NO ____

If YES,

b. **For this current episode, how many times have you seen a doctor for these symptoms since your fear or belief that you have _______ began?**

____

c. **What have been the findings of these medical evaluations?**

____

d. **If the doctor tells you that s/he can find nothing wrong, do you feel reassured that you do not have a physical disease?**

YES ____ NO ____

If YES, **How long does this reassurance last?** ______________________________

Does this reassurance "wear off" such that you still believe that you are physically ill?

YES ____ NO ____

3a. **Currently, how strongly do you believe that you have** ________ (0-100 scale where 0 = not at all and 100 = completely)?

________ %

b. **Is there any evidence that you can think of that might indicate to you that you do not have** _________**?**

YES ____ NO ____

If YES, have patient specify: ____

4. **In what ways has this fear or belief that you have ______ interfered with your life (e.g., daily routine, job, social activities)?; How much are you bothered about having the fear/belief of having ______?**

____

____

Rate interference: ___________ distress: ___________

0----------1----------2----------3----------4----------5----------6----------7----------8
None Mild Moderate Severe Very severe

5a. **For this current period of time, when did the fear/belief that you had ________ become a problem in that you became preoccupied with this fear/belief, you were bothered by this preoccupation, or it interfered with your life in some way?** (Note: if patient is vague in date of onset, attempt to ascertain more specific information, e.g., by linking onset to objective life events.)

____

Date of Onset: ___________ Month ___________ Year

If uncertain about duration, **Have you been bothered by the preoccupation that you have ______ for at least the past 6 months?**

YES ____ NO ____

b. **Can you recall anything that might have led to this problem?** ____________________

____

____

6. **Besides this current period when you feared/believed that you've had ______, have there been other, separate periods of time before this when you have had the same problems (perhaps involving a different disease or illness)?**

YES ____ NO ____

If YES, go back and ask 2b. and 2c. from INITIAL INQUIRY (p. 71).

If NO, skip to SOMATIZATION DISORDER (p. 76).

III. PAST EPISODE

Now I want to ask you a series of questions about the past period of time when you feared or believed that you had a serious disease or illness that began roughly in ________ and ended roughly in ________ (specify months/ years).

List diseases/illnesses of inquiry: ______________________________

1a. **Did you experience certain bodily symptoms or sensations that were associated with your fear or belief that you had ________** (specify disease)**?**

YES ____ NO ____

If YES,

b. **What symptoms did you experience?**

____

c. **How often did these symptoms occur?**

____

2a. **Did you see a doctor to determine whether you had _______ or any other physical illness?**

YES ____ NO ____

If YES,

b. **During that past episode, how many times did you see a doctor for these symptoms?**

____

c. **What were the findings of these medical evaluations?**

____

d. **If the doctor told you that s/he could find nothing wrong, did you feel reassured that you did not have a physical disease?**

YES ____ NO ____

If YES, How long did this reassurance last? ____________________

Did this reassurance "wear off" such that you still believed that you were physically ill?

YES ____ NO ____

3a. **During that time, how strongly did you believe that you had ________** (0-100 scale where 0 = not at all and 100 = completely)?

________ %

b. **Were you able to consider any contradictory evidence that indicated to you that you might not have had _________?**

YES ____ NO ____

4. **In what ways did this fear or belief that you had _______ interfere with your life (e.g., daily routine, job, social activities)?; How much were you bothered about having the fear/belief of having ______?**

____

____

Rate interference: ___________ distress: ___________

0----------1----------2----------3----------4----------5----------6----------7----------8

None Mild Moderate Severe Very severe

5a. **During that period of time in ________** (year), **when did the fear/belief that you had ________ become a problem in that you became preoccupied with this fear/belief, you were bothered by this preoccupation, or it interfered with your life in some way?** (Note: if patient is vague in date of onset, attempt to ascertain more specific information, e.g., by linking onset to objective life events.)

____

Date of Onset: ___________ Month ___________ Year

b. **Can you recall anything that might have led to this problem?** ____________________

____

____

6a. **When was this no longer a problem, in that you were no longer preoccupied with having ________, and the fear/belief of having this physical disease no longer bothered you or interfered with your life?**

Date of Remission: __________ Month __________ Year

If uncertain about duration, **During that period, were you been bothered by the preoccupation that you had ______ for at least 6 months?**

YES ____ NO ____

b. **Can you recall any reasons why you were no longer preoccupied with the fear or belief of having ________?**

____

____

7. **Prior to/after this past period when you feared/believed that you had ______, have there been other, separate periods of time that we haven't covered when you have had the same problems (perhaps involving a different disease or illness)?**

YES ____ NO ____

If YES, go back and ask 2b. and 2c. from INITIAL INQUIRY (p. 71).

If NO, skip to SOMATIZATION DISORDER (p. 76).

SOMATIZATION DISORDER

I. INITIAL INQUIRY

1a. **Have you had a lot of different physical problems in your life?**

YES ____ NO ____

If YES,

b. **Over the past several years, have these physical problems prompted you to see the doctor on many occasions or have they significantly interfered with your life (e.g., job, social activities)?**

YES ____ NO ____

If YES, specify: ____

c. **Over the past several years, have doctors often had difficulty either diagnosing the source of these symptoms or treating these symptoms effectively?**

YES ____ NO ____

If YES, specify: ____

****

If YES to 1a. and 1b. or 1c., or uncertain, continue inquiry.
Otherwise, skip to **MIXED ANXIETY-DEPRESSION** (p. 79).

****

II. CURRENT EPISODE

1. Physical Symptoms

Rate each symptom using the scales and suggested inquiries listed below. Obtain SEVERITY rating to establish presence and severity of each physical symptom. If symptom has occurred at some time during the course of the disorder, obtain AGE OF ONSET and NONORGANIC/EXCESS ratings.

SEVERITY (0-8 scale):

Over the past several years, have you had a lot of trouble with _______?; How often have you experienced __________?

0----------1----------2----------3----------4----------5----------6----------7----------8

0	2	4	6	8
Never/ None	Rarely/ Mild	Occasionally/ Moderate	Frequently/ Severe	Constantly/ Very severe

AGE OF ONSET (Yes = Onset $<$ 30; No = Onset $>$ 30):

How old were you when these symptoms began?; If unsure: **Did these symptoms begin before you were 30?**

NOT DUE TO OR IN EXCESS OF A KNOWN MEDICAL CONDITION (Yes/No):

Over the past several years, have doctors often had difficulty either diagnosing the source of these symptoms or treating these symptoms effectively?

	SEVERITY	ONSET < 30	NONORGANIC/ EXCESS
A. Pain symptoms:			
Head pain	____	Y N	Y N
Abdominal pain	____	Y N	Y N
Back pain	____	Y N	Y N
Joint pain	____	Y N	Y N
Pain in extremities	____	Y N	Y N
Chest pain	____	Y N	Y N
Rectal pain	____	Y N	Y N
Pain during sexual intercourse	____	Y N	Y N
Painful menstruation	____	Y N	Y N
Painful urination	____	Y N	Y N
B. Gastrointestinal symptoms:			
Nausea	____	Y N	Y N
Diarrhea	____	Y N	Y N
Bloating	____	Y N	Y N
Vomiting (not due to pregnancy)	____	Y N	Y N
Intolerance of several different foods	____	Y N	Y N
C. Pseudoneurologic symptoms:			
Blindness	____	Y N	Y N
Double vision	____	Y N	Y N
Deafness	____	Y N	Y N
Loss of touch or pain sensation	____	Y N	Y N
Hallucinations	____	Y N	Y N
Aphonia	____	Y N	Y N
Impaired coordination or balance	____	Y N	Y N
Paralysis or localized weakness	____	Y N	Y N
Difficulty swallowing	____	Y N	Y N
Difficulty breathing	____	Y N	Y N
Urinary retention	____	Y N	Y N
Seizures	____	Y N	Y N
Amnesia	____	Y N	Y N
Loss of consciousness (other than fainting)	____	Y N	Y N
D. Sexual symptoms-Males:			
Sexual indifference	____	Y N	Y N
Erectile/ejaculatory dysfunction	____	Y N	Y N
E. Sexual symptoms-Females:			
Sexual indifference	____	Y N	Y N
Irregular menses	____	Y N	Y N
Excessive menstrual bleeding	____	Y N	Y N
Vomiting throughout pregnancy	____	Y N	Y N

2. **In what ways have these physical problems interfered with your life (e.g., job, social activities, depletion of finances due to numerous doctor visits)?; How much have you been bothered by these difficulties?**

____

____

Rate interference: __________ distress: __________

0----------1----------2----------3----------4----------5----------6----------7----------8

None | Mild | Moderate | Severe | Very severe

3a. **When did these physical difficulties first become a problem for you in that they prompted your initial doctor visits or they began to interfere with your life in some way?** (Note: if patient is vague in date of onset, attempt to ascertain more specific information, e.g., by linking onset to objective life events.)

____

Date of Onset: __________ Month __________ Year

b. **Can you recall anything that might have led to this problem?** ____________________

____

____

MIXED ANXIETY-DEPRESSIVE DISORDER

****

DO NOT ADMINISTER this section if the patient:

(a) Currently meets criteria for any Anxiety or Mood Disorder (including disorders in partial remission), Adjustment Disorder with Anxiety, or Adjustment Disorder with Mixed Anxiety and Depressed Mood

(b) Has a past (or current) diagnosis of Major Depression, Dysthymic Disorder, Panic Disorder, or Generalized Anxiety Disorder

****

I. INITIAL INQUIRY

1a. **Currently, do you often have days when you feel somewhat down or depressed or maybe anxious or keyed up?**

YES ____ NO ____

If YES, skip to 2a.

b. If NO, **Have you ever had a period of one month or more when you felt somewhat down or depressed or anxious or keyed up?**

YES ____ NO ____

If YES, **When was the most recent time this occurred?**

____

****

If YES to either 1a. or 1b., or uncertain, continue inquiry.
Otherwise, skip to **ALCOHOL ABUSE** (p. 84)

****

2a. **Besides this current/most recent period of time when you felt somewhat down or anxious, have there been other, separate periods of time when you experienced similar feelings?**

YES ____ NO ____

If NO, skip to CURRENT EPISODE.

b. **So prior to this current/most recent period of time when you have been feeling somewhat down or anxious, there was a considerable period of time when you were not feeling this way at all?**

YES ____ NO ____

c. **How much time separated these periods?; When did this/these separate period(s) occur?**

____

II. CURRENT EPISODE

If evidence of a discrete past episode, preface inquiry in this section with: **Now I want to ask you a series of questions about this current period of time when you felt somewhat down and anxious, that began roughly in** __________ (specify month/year).

1. **What percentage of the days over the past month have you felt down, depressed, anxious, or keyed up?**

   ________%

   If uncertain, **Have you felt this way more days than not over the past month?**

   YES ____ NO ____

2. **Over the past month, have you often experienced** __________ **while feeling down, depressed, anxious, or keyed up?**

   0----------1----------2----------3----------4----------5----------6----------7----------8
   None Mild Moderate Severe Very severe

   SEVERITY

   a. difficulty concentrating or mind going blank ____
   b. difficulty falling or staying asleep; restless, unsatisfying sleep ____
   c. fatigue or low energy ____
   d. irritability ____
   e. worry over day-to-day matters ____
   f. moved to tears easily ____
   g. hypervigilance ____
   h. anticipating the worst ____
   i. pessimism about the future ____
   j. low self-esteem; feelings of worthlessness ____

3. **In what ways have these symptoms interfered with your life (e.g., daily routine, job, social activities)?; How much are you bothered about having these symptoms?**

   ____

   ____

   Rate interference: __________ distress: __________

   0----------1----------2----------3----------4----------5----------6----------7----------8
   None Mild Moderate Severe Very severe

4. **Over this entire current period of time when you've been experiencing these feelings, have you been regularly taking any types of drugs** (Include drugs of abuse, medication.)?

   YES ____ NO ____

   Specify (type; amount; dates of use): ________________________________

   ____

5. **During this current period of time when you've been having these feelings, have you had any physical condition** (e.g., pregnancy, hypothyroidism, hypoglycemia)?

   YES ____ NO ____

   Specify (type; date of onset/remission): ________________________________

   ____

6a. **For this current period of time, when did the symptoms of anxiety and depression become a problem in that they occurred persistently (i.e., occurred nearly every day), you were bothered by these symptoms, or they interfered with your life in some way?** (Note: if patient is vague in date of onset, attempt to ascertain more specific information, e.g., by linking onset to objective life events.)

____

Date of Onset: __________ Month __________ Year

b. **Can you recall anything that might have led to this problem?** ____________________

____

____

c. **Were you under any type of stress during this time?**

YES ___ NO ___

What was happening in your life at the time?

____

____

Were you experiencing any difficulties or changes in:

(1) **Family/relationships?** ____________________

(2) **Work/school?** ____________________

(3) **Finances?** ____________________

(4) **Legal matters?** ____________________

(5) **Health** (self/others)? ____________________

7. **Besides this current period of time, have there been other, separate periods when you have felt somewhat down or anxious more days than not for a period of a month or more?**

YES ___ NO ___

If YES, go back and ask 2b. and 2c. from INITIAL INQUIRY (p. 79).

If NO, skip to ALCOHOL ABUSE (p. 84).

III. PAST EPISODE

Now I want to ask you a series of questions about the past period(s) of anxiety/depression that began roughly in _____ and ended roughly in _____ (specify months/years).

1. **During that period of time in ________** (years), **on average, what percentage of the days per month did you feel down, depressed, anxious, or keyed up?**

________%

If uncertain, **On average, did you feel this way more days than not during this period?**

YES ___ NO ___

2. **During that period of time in ______ (years), did you often experience __________ while feeling down, depressed, anxious, or keyed up?**

0----------1----------2----------3----------4----------5----------6----------7----------8
None Mild Moderate Severe Very severe

	SEVERITY
a. difficulty concentrating or mind going blank	____
b. difficulty falling or staying asleep; restless, unsatisfying sleep	____
c. fatigue or low energy	____
d. irritability	____
e. worry over day-to-day matters	____
f. moved to tears easily	____
g. hypervigilance	____
h. anticipating the worst	____
i. pessimism about the future	____
j. low self-esteem; feelings of worthlessness	____

3. **In what ways did these symptoms interfere with your life (e.g., daily routine, job, social activities)?; How much were you bothered about having these symptoms?**

____

____

Rate interference: ___________ distress: ___________

0----------1----------2----------3----------4----------5----------6----------7----------8
None Mild Moderate Severe Very severe

4. **Over that entire period of time when you were experiencing these feelings, did you regularly take any types of drugs?** (Include drugs of abuse, medication.)

YES ____ NO ____

Specify (type; amount; dates of use): ____

____

5. **During that period of time, did you have any physical condition** (e.g., pregnancy, hypothyroidism, hypoglycemia)?

YES ____ NO ____

Specify (type; date of onset/remission): ____

____

6a. **For that past period of time, when did the symptoms of anxiety and depression become a problem in that they occurred persistently (i.e., occurred nearly every day), you were bothered by these symptoms, or they interfered with your life in some way?** (Note: if patient is vague in date of onset, attempt to ascertain more specific information, e.g., by linking onset to objective life events.)

____

Date of Onset: ___________ Month ___________ Year

b. **Can you recall anything that might have led to this problem?** ______________________

____

____

c. **Were you under any type of stress during this time?**

YES ____ NO ____

What was happening in your life at the time?

____

____

Were you experiencing any difficulties or changes in:

(1) **Family/relationships?** ______________________________

(2) **Work/school?** ______________________________

(3) **Finances?** ______________________________

(4) **Legal matters?** ______________________________

(5) **Health** (self/others)? ______________________________

7a. **When were the symptoms of anxiety and depression no longer a problem, in that they no longer occurred persistently, you were not bothered by these symptoms, and they did not interfere with your life?**

Date of Remission: __________ Month __________ Year

b. **Can you recall any reasons why these feelings subsided?**

____

____

8. **Prior to/after this past period, have there been other, separate periods of time that we haven't covered when you have had the same problems?**

YES ____ NO ____

If YES, go back and ask 2b. and 2c. from INITIAL INQUIRY (p. 79).

If NO, skip to ALCOHOL ABUSE (p. 84).

ALCOHOL ABUSE/DEPENDENCE

I. INITIAL INQUIRY

1a. **Currently, how much alcohol do you typically drink?** (Specify number, type, and amount of alcoholic beverage used and indicate time period; e.g., "three 12 oz. beers per week.")

____

____

If patient currently drinks alcohol, skip to 2.

b. **Has there ever been a period of time in your life when you drank alcohol?**

YES ____ NO ____

If YES,

How much alcohol did you typically drink? (Specify number, type, and amount of alcoholic beverage used and indicate time period, e.g., "three 12 oz. beers per week.")

____

____

When was the most recent period of time when you drank?

____

****

If no evidence of current or past alcohol use,
Skip to **SUBSTANCE ABUSE** (p. 88).

****

2. Current and Past Alcohol Abuse

Inquire about CURRENT or PAST alcohol abuse as indicated by presence of alcohol use obtained from the above screening questions. If there is evidence of current alcohol abuse, inquire for the presence of prior, discrete episodes of disturbance (e.g., "**Since this problem began, have there been periods of time when you were not bothered by it?**"). Rate the frequency of each symptom using the scale below. If the symptom is present, provide further information as necessary.

0----------1----------2	----------3----------4	----------5----------6	----------7----------8
Never/ None	Rarely/ Mild	Occasionally/ Moderate	Frequently/ Severe	Constantly/ Very severe

0----------1----------2----------3----------4----------5----------6----------7----------8

0	2	4	6	8
Never/ None	Rarely/ Mild	Occasionally/ Moderate	Frequently/ Severe	Constantly/ Very severe

CURRENT:
Over the past year, has your drinking resulted in any problems such as:

PAST:
During that time, did your drinking result in any problems such as:

	FREQUENCY/SEVERITY	
	CURRENT	PAST
a. **Poor work [school] attendance or performance?**		
______________________________	____	____
b. **Legal problems (e.g., DWIs, disorderly conduct)?**		
______________________________	____	____

	FREQUENCY/SEVERITY	
	CURRENT	PAST
c. **Arguments with family or friends about when or how much you drink?** ______________	____	____
d. **Drank at times when it may have been physically hazardous to you (e.g., while driving, against medical advice)?** ______________	____	____
e. **Drank to attempt to reduce or avoid a negative mood state such as anxiety or depression?** ______________	____	____

****

If no evidence of current or past alcohol abuse,
Skip to **SUBSTANCE ABUSE** (p. 88).

****

II. ALCOHOL ABUSE/DEPENDENCE (Current and Past Episodes)

1. Alcohol Dependence

The following items pertain to the diagnostic criteria for Alcohol Dependence. Regardless of whether the patient meets criteria for Alcohol Dependence, administer this entire section if there is evidence that the patient meets criteria for Alcohol Abuse.

Inquire about CURRENT or PAST alcohol dependence as indicated by presence of alcohol use obtained from the above questions. If there is evidence of current alcohol abuse or dependence, inquire for the presence of prior, discrete episodes of disturbance (e.g., "**Since this problem began, have there been periods of time when you were not bothered by it?**"). Rate the frequency of each symptom using the scale below. If the symptom is present, provide further information as necessary.

0----------1----------2----------3----------4----------5----------6----------7----------8

0	2	4	6	8
Never/ None	Rarely/ Mild	Occasionally/ Moderate	Frequently/ Severe	Constantly/ Very severe

CURRENT: **At any point during the current time, has your drinking resulted in:**

PAST: **During that time in ________ (years), did your drinking result in:**

	FREQUENCY/SEVERITY	
	CURRENT	PAST
a. **Need to drink a lot more to become intoxicated or achieve the effect you desired?** ______________	____	____
b. **Notable decrease in effects of drinking the same amount of alcohol?** ______________	____	____
c. **Unpleasant symptoms when you stopped drinking for awhile (e.g., sweating, increased heart rate, tremor, sleep difficulties, stomach distress, hallucinations, agitation, anxiety, seizures)?** ______________	____	____

0----------1----------2----------3----------4----------5----------6----------7----------8

Never/ None	Rarely/ Mild	Occasionally/ Moderate	Frequently/ Severe	Constantly/ Very severe

FREQUENCY/SEVERITY

CURRENT PAST

d. **Need to use a different substance to reduce unpleasant symptoms produced by discontinuing alcohol?**

__________________________ _____ _____

e. **Drink larger amounts or over longer periods of time than you intended to?**

__________________________ _____ _____

f. **Found it difficult to cut down or control your drinking?**

__________________________ _____ _____

g. **Spent a considerable amount of time obtaining or using alcohol or recovering from its effects?**

__________________________ _____ _____

h. **Gave up or cut back on work, leisure activities, or social relationships because of the alcohol?**

__________________________ _____ _____

i. **Continued to drink despite the fact that you knew you had a medical or emotional problem that the alcohol was creating or making worse?**

__________________________ _____ _____

2. **Overall, how much did/does your drinking interfere with your life (e.g., daily routine, job, social activities)?; How much are/were you bothered by your drinking?**

C: __________________________

P: __________________________

CURRENT: Rate interference: __________ distress: __________
PAST: Rate interference: __________ distress: __________

0----------1----------2----------3----------4----------5----------6----------7----------8

None Mild Moderate Severe Very severe

3a. **For the current/past period of time, when did your drinking become a problem in that the amount or occasions when you drank became problematic and/or the alcohol began to produce some of the other difficulties we just talked about?** (Note: if patient is vague in date of onset, attempt to ascertain more specific information, e.g., by linking onset to objective life events.)

C: __________________________

P: __________________________

Date of Onset: CURRENT: __________ Month __________ Year
PAST: __________ Month __________ Year

b. **Can you recall anything that might have led to this problem?**

C: __________________________

P: __________________________

c. **Were you under any type of stress during this time?**

YES ____ NO ____

What was happening in your life at the time?

C: ____________________

P: ____________________

Were you experiencing any difficulties or changes in:

(1) **Family/relationships?** C: ____________________

P: ____________________

(2) **Work/school?** C: ____________________

P: ____________________

(3) **Finances?** C: ____________________

P: ____________________

(4) **Legal matters?** C: ____________________

P: ____________________

(5) **Health** (self/others)? C: ____________________

P: ____________________

If evidence of CURRENT Alcohol Abuse/Dependence only, skip to 5.

4a. **When did you stop drinking?; When were you able to cut back or control your drinking such that it no longer resulted in any of the difficulties we just talked about?**

Date of Remission: __________ Month __________ Year

b. **Can you recall any reasons why this problem subsided?**

____

____

5. **Prior to/after this current/past period, have there been other, separate periods of time that we haven't covered when you have had problems with drinking?**

YES ____ NO ____

If YES, go back and ask Item 2 from INITIAL INQUIRY (p. 84).

If NO, skip to SUBSTANCE ABUSE (p. 88).

SUBSTANCE ABUSE/DEPENDENCE

I. INITIAL INQUIRY

1. Caffeine Use

a. **Currently, how much caffeine do you typically drink?** (Specify number, type, and amount of caffeinated beverage used and indicate time period; e.g., "three cups of coffee per day.")

____

____

b. **Has your caffeine use caused you any difficulties (e.g., anxiety, sleep difficulties, physical symptoms such as GI disturbances, agitation, headaches)?**

YES ____ NO ____

If YES, specify: ____

2a. **Besides alcohol or caffeine, have you ever used any other substances such as marijuana or cocaine?**

YES ____ NO ____

b. **Have you ever used certain prescription or nonprescription medications (e.g., anxiolytics, cough remedies) in excessive amounts or at a frequency or dosage that was higher than that prescribed by your doctor?**

YES ____ NO ____

****

If no evidence of caffeine or other substance abuse,
Skip to **PSYCHOSIS** (p. 93).

****

3. Other Substance Use

Note: If evidence of caffeine abuse only (i.e., NO to 2a. and 2b.), this item may be skipped after 3a.

Ascertain if patient is currently (past year) or has ever used any of the following substances. Specify particular substances of use. Inquire about frequency of usage and for PAST use, indicate the time period over which the substance use occurred.

CURRENT: **In the past year, have you used/taken ______?; How often?**

PAST: **Have you ever used/taken _____?; How often?; During what time period?**

	CURRENT	PAST
a. Excessive caffeine use ______________________________	Y N	Y N
b. Amphetamines ______________________________	Y N	Y N
c. Marijuana, hashish ______________________________	Y N	Y N

	CURRENT	PAST
d. Cocaine ______	Y N	Y N
e. Hallucinogens (e.g., LSD, PCP, mushrooms) ______	Y N	Y N
f. Inhalants ______	Y N	Y N
g. Opioids (e.g., heroin) ______	Y N	Y N
h. Barbituates ______	Y N	Y N
i. Excessive use/misuse of prescription medications (e.g., anxiolytics, hypnotics) ______	Y N	Y N
j. Excessive use/misuse of nonprescription medications ______	Y N	Y N

****

If no evidence of caffeine or other substance use/abuse,
Skip to **PSYCHOSIS** (p. 93).

****

II. SUBSTANCE ABUSE

Specify substance(s) of inquiry: ______________________________

Inquire about CURRENT or PAST substance abuse as indicated by presence of use obtained from the above screening questions. If there is evidence of current abuse, inquire for the presence of prior, discrete episodes of disturbance (e.g., "**Since this problem began, have there been periods of time when you were not bothered by it?**"). Rate the frequency of each symptom using the scale below. If the symptom is present, provide further information as necessary.

0----------1----------2----------3----------4----------5----------6----------7----------8

0	2	4	6	8
Never/ None	Rarely/ Mild	Occasionally/ Moderate	Frequently/ Severe	Constantly/ Very severe

CURRENT: **Over the past year, has use of ______ resulted in any problems such as:**

PAST: **During that time, did use of ______ result in any problems such as:**

	FREQUENCY/SEVERITY CURRENT	PAST
a. **Poor work [school] attendance or performance?** ______	____	____
b. **Legal problems (e.g., DWIs, disorderly conduct)?** ______	____	____

0----------1----------2----------3----------4----------5----------6----------7----------8

Never/ None	Rarely/ Mild	Occasionally/ Moderate	Frequently/ Severe	Constantly/ Very severe

FREQUENCY/SEVERITY
CURRENT PAST

c. **Arguments with family or friends about when or how much you of the substance you use?**

_______________________________________ _____ _____

d. **Used _____ at times when it may have been physically hazardous to you (e.g., while driving, against medical advice)?**

_______________________________________ _____ _____

e. **Used ______ excessively to attempt to reduce or avoid a negative mood state such as anxiety or depression?**

_______________________________________ _____ _____

****

If no evidence of current or past substance abuse,
Skip to **PSYCHOSIS** (p. 93).

****

III. SUBSTANCE ABUSE/DEPENDENCE (Current and Past Episodes)

1. Substance Dependence

The following items pertain to the diagnostic criteria for Substance Dependence. Regardless of whether the patient meets criteria for Substance Dependence, administer this entire section if there is evidence that the patient meets criteria for Substance Abuse.

Inquire about CURRENT or PAST substance dependence as indicated by presence of substance use obtained from the above questions. If there is evidence of current substance abuse or dependence, inquire for the presence of prior, discrete episodes of disturbance (e.g., **"Since this problem began, have there been periods of time when you were not bothered by it?"**). Rate the frequency of each symptom using the scale below. If the symptom is present, provide further information as necessary.

0----------1----------2----------3----------4----------5----------6----------7----------8

Never/ None	Rarely/ Mild	Occasionally/ Moderate	Frequently/ Severe	Constantly/ Very severe

CURRENT: **At any point during the current time, has use of ____ resulted in:**

PAST: **During that time in ________ (years), did use of _____ result in:**

FREQUENCY/SEVERITY
CURRENT PAST

a. **Need to take a lot more of ______ to become intoxicated or achieve the effect you desired?**

_______________________________________ _____ _____

b. **A notable decrease in effects of using the same amount of _____?**

_______________________________________ _____ _____

	FREQUENCY/SEVERITY	
	CURRENT	PAST
c. **Unpleasant symptoms when you stopped using ______ for a while?** ________________	____	____
d. **Need to use a different substance to reduce unpleasant symptoms produced by discontinuing ______?** ________________	____	____
e. **Took larger amounts of _____ or took it over longer periods of time than you intended to?** ________________	____	____
f. **Found it difficult to cut down or control your use of _____?** ________________	____	____
g. **Spent a considerable amount of time obtaining or using _____ or recovering from its effects?** ________________	____	____
h. **Gave up or cut back on work, leisure activities, or social relationships because of _____?** ________________	____	____
i. **Continued to use _____ despite the fact that you knew you had a medical or emotional problem that it was creating or making worse?** ________________	____	____

2. **Overall, how much did/does taking _____ interfere with your life (e.g., daily routine, job, social activities)?; How much are/were you bothered by your use of it?**

C: ____

P: ____

CURRENT: Rate interference: __________ distress: __________
PAST: Rate interference: __________ distress: __________

0----------1----------2----------3----------4----------5----------6----------7----------8
None Mild Moderate Severe Very severe

3a. **For the current/past period of time, when did your use of _____ become a problem in that the amount or occasions when you used it became problematic and/or _____ began to produce some of the other difficulties we just talked about?** (Note: if patient is vague in date of onset, attempt to ascertain more specific information, e.g., by linking onset to objective life events.)

C: ____

P: ____

Date of Onset: CURRENT: __________ Month __________ Year
PAST: __________ Month __________ Year

b. **Can you recall anything that might have led to this problem?**

C: ____

P: ____

c. **Were you under any type of stress during this time?**

YES ____ NO ____

What was happening in your life at the time?

C: ____________________

P: ____________________

Were you experiencing any difficulties or changes in:

(1) **Family/relationships?** C: ____________________

P: ____________________

(2) **Work/school?** C: ____________________

P: ____________________

(3) **Finances?** C: ____________________

P: ____________________

(4) **Legal matters?** C: ____________________

P: ____________________

(5) **Health** (self/others)? C: ____________________

P: ____________________

If evidence of CURRENT Substance Abuse/Dependence only, skip to 5.

4a. **When did you stop using _____?; When were you able to cut back or control your use of _____ such that it no longer resulted in any of the difficulties we just talked about?**

Date of Remission: ___________ Month ___________ Year

b. **Can you recall any reasons why this problem subsided?**

____

____

5. **Prior to/after this current/past period, have there been other, separate periods of time that we haven't covered when you have had problems with the use of ______ or other substances?**

YES ____ NO ____

If YES, go back and ask Item 3 from INITIAL INQUIRY (p. 88).

If NO, skip to PSYCHOSIS (p. 93).

NONORGANIC PSYCHOSIS/CONVERSION SYMPTOMS

1. **Have you ever experienced a loss or change in your physical functioning such as paralysis, seizures, or severe pain?**

   YES ____ NO ____

   If YES, specify details and time periods: ______________________________

   ____

   ____

2. **Has there ever been a period of time when you had strange of unusual experiences such as:**

   a. **Hearing or seeing things that other people didn't notice?** YES ____ NO ____

   b. **Hear voices or conversations when no one was around?** YES ____ NO ____

   c. **Visions that no one else saw?** YES ____ NO ____

   d. **Had the feeling that something odd was going on around you, that people were doing things to test you or antagonize or hurt you so that you felt you had to be on guard constantly?** YES ____ NO ____

   If YES to any of above, specify details and time periods: ______________________________

   ____

   ____

FAMILY HISTORY OF PSYCHOLOGICAL DISORDERS

1. **Has anyone in your immediate, biological family (e.g., mother, father, siblings) ever been treated or hospitalized for anxiety, depression, substance use, or other such problems, or had any such problems but did not seek treatment?**

   YES ____ NO ____

   If YES, specify: ______________________________

2. Inquire about each of the following (type of disorder, dates of occurrence, nature of treatment):

	Disorder	Dates	Treatment
a. Mother			
b. Father			
c. Sister(s)			
d. Brother(s)			
e. Maternal grandparents			
f. Paternal grandparents			
g. Other (e.g., aunts, uncles)			

MEDICAL/TREATMENT HISTORY

I. HISTORY OF PSYCHOLOGICAL/PSYCHIATRIC TREATMENT

1a. **Have you ever been hospitalized for anxiety, depression, substance use, or any other emotional problem?**

YES ____ NO ____

Date	Hospital/Doctor	Reason	Treatment/Medication

b. **Have you ever received any outpatient treatment or evaluations for any emotional or personal difficulties?**

YES ____ NO ____

Date	Clinic/Doctor	Reason	Treatment/Medication

2a. **Are you currently taking any medications for anxiety, depression, or any other emotional problem?** (Include sleep medications.)

YES ____ NO ____

Date	Clinic/Doctor	Reason	Medication/Dose

b. **Have you ever taken any medications for anxiety, depression, or any other emotional problem?** (Include sleep medications.)

YES ____ NO ____

Date	Clinic/Doctor	Reason	Medication/Dose

If CURRENT or PAST history of psychotropic medication use, ask:

c. **Have you ever experienced problems with these medications such as side effects, withdrawal problems, etc.?**

YES ____ NO ____

If YES, specify: ______________________________

II. MEDICAL HISTORY

1a. **What is your height?** __________ b. **What is your weight?** __________

2a. **Do you have a physician/clinic that you see regularly to receive medical care, physical examinations, etc.?**

YES ____ NO ____

Name/address of physician or clinic:

____

____

b. **Are you currently being treated for any physical disease or condition?**

YES ____ NO ____

If YES, specify: ______________________________

3a. **When was your last physical exam?** ______________________

b. **What were the results of this exam?** ______________________

4a. **Have you ever had to be hospitalized for a physical problem?**

YES ____ NO ____

Date	Hospital/Doctor	Reason	Comments/Complications

b. **Have you ever had surgery, or been advised to have surgery?**

YES ____ NO ____

Date	Hospital/Doctor	Reason	Comments/Complications

c. **Have you ever had a concussion or any head injury?**

YES ____ NO ____

Date	Hospital/Doctor	Treatment	Comments/Complications

3. **Have you ever been diagnosed with any of the following:**

	Yes	No	Date	Comments
a. Diabetes	___	___		
b. Heart problems	___	___		
c. High/low blood pressure	___	___		

	Yes	No	Date	Comments
d. Epilepsy	___	___		
e. Cancer	___	___		
f. Thyroid disease	___	___		
g. Other hormonal problem	___	___		
h. Asthma	___	___		
i. Other respiratory problem	___	___		
j. Migraines	___	___		
k. Stroke	___	___		
l. Ulcers/GI problems	___	___		
m. Blood disorders	___	___		
n. HIV/AIDS	___	___		
o. **Any other disease?**	___	___		

p. **Is there a family history (e.g., father, mother, siblings) of any of these problems** (e.g., hypertension, heart disease, cancer)?

YES ____ NO ____

If YES, specify: ______________________________

4. **Do you have any allergies (hay fever, penicillin, medications, etc.)?**

YES ____ NO ____

If YES, specify: ______________________________

5. **Are you a smoker?**

YES ____ NO ____

If YES, **Packs/day?**: ____________ **How many years?** ____________

6. **Have you had any of the following tests in the last five years?; Did these tests indicate any abnormalities?**

	Yes	No	Date	Results
a. Electrocardiogram (EKG)	___	___		
b. EEG, brain scan, EMI	___	___		
c. CT scan or similar	___	___		
d. Chest X-ray	___	___		
e. Blood test	___	___		
f. Urine test	___	___		

7. FEMALES:

a. **Date last menstrual period began:** ________________

b. **Any reason to be believe you may be pregnant?** YES ____ NO ____

c. **History of any gynecological problems, miscarriages, etc.?**

YES ____ NO ____

If YES, specify: ______________________________

HAMILTON SCALES (Optional)

1. All ratings are for the PAST MONTH.

2. Adjacent anxiety and depression items cover similar symptom areas, and can be rated together. Suggested phrasing is included for some items.

3. Hamilton Depression items are scored on the basis of the list of descriptors which accompanies each item.

4. Hamilton Anxiety items are rated on the following scale:

0	1	2	3	4
None	Mild	Moderate	Severe	Very severe

In arriving at symptom ratings, the examiner should take into account both the patient's general level of symptomatology and the degree to which phobic or panic symptoms interfere with everyday functioning. For example, if panics or exposures to feared situations are frequent, then the overall rating should be higher than if the panics or exposures are infrequent.

SCORING FOR HAMILTON ANXIETY:

0---------------1---------------2---------------3---------------4
None Mild Moderate Severe Very severe

HAMILTON ANXIETY	SEVERITY	HAMILTON DEPRESSION (circle item which applies)
1. Anxious Mood: **Do you worry about a lot of things, a lot of minor problems?** 1 m Worries .... ___ Anticipation of the worst.................. ___ Apprehension.......... ___ Irritability.......... ___	___	10. Anxiety Psychic: 1 No difficulty 2 Subjective tension and irritability 3 Worrying about minor matters 4 Apprehensive attitude apparent in face or speech 5 Fears expressed without questioning
2. Tension: 1 m Feelings of tension... ___ Fatigability.......... ___ Inability to relax, keyed up.............. ___ Startle response...... ___ Moved to tears easily. ___ Trembling............. ___ Feelings of restlessness.......... ___	___	
3. Fears: Rate any specific fear on severity and frequency of exposure 1 m ___	___	

SCORING FOR HAMILTON ANXIETY:

0---------------1---------------2---------------3---------------4
None Mild Moderate Severe Very severe

HAMILTON ANXIETY	SEVERITY	HAMILTON DEPRESSION (circle item which applies)
4. Insomnia: **How is your sleep?** (1 m) Difficulty in falling asleep................ ___ Broken sleep.......... ___ Unsatisfying sleep fatigue on waking..... ___ Dreams................ ___ Nightmares............ ___ Night terrors......... ___	___	4. Insomnia Early: 1 No difficulty falling asleep 2 Complains of occasional difficulty falling asleep (i.e., more than 1/2 hour) 3 Complains of nightly difficulty falling asleep 5. Insomnia Middle: 1 No difficulty 2 Patient complains of being restless and disturbed during the night 3 Waking during the night - any getting out of bed rates 3 (except for purposes of voiding) 6. Insomnia Late: 1 No difficulty 2 Waking in early hours of the AM but goes back to sleep 3 Unable to fall asleep again if gets out of bed
5. Intellectual, cognitive: **Does the anxiety break up your concentration while at work, reading, watching TV, etc.?** (1 m) Difficulty in concentration, mind going blank........... ___ Poor memory........... ___	___	8. Retardation: Slowness of thought and speech: impaired ability to concentrate: decreased motor activity 1 Normal speech and thought 2 Slight retardation at interview 3 Obvious retardation at interview 4 Interview difficult 5 Complete stupor

SCORING FOR HAMILTON ANXIETY:

0---------------1---------------2---------------3---------------4
None Mild Moderate Severe Very severe

HAMILTON ANXIETY	SEVERITY	HAMILTON DEPRESSION (circle item which applies)
7. General somatic, muscular: (1 m) Muscular pains and aches................. ___ Muscular stiffness.... ___ Clonic jerk........... ___ Muscular twitchings... ___ Grinding of teeth..... ___ Unsteady voice........ ___	____	13. Somatic Symptoms General: Heaviness in limbs, back or head. Backaches, headaches, muscle aches. Loss of energy and fatigability 1 None 2 Slight 3 Clearly present
8. General somatic, sensory: (1 m) Tinnitus.............. ___ Blurring of vision.... ___ Hot and cold flashes, ___ chills................ ___ Feeings of weakness... ___ Pricking sensations... ___	____	
9. Cardiovascular Symptoms: (1 m) Tachycardia........... ___ Palpitations.......... ___ Pain in chest......... ___ Throbbing of vessels.. ___ Fainting feelings..... ___ Missing beat.......... ___	____	
10. Respiratory Symptoms: (1 m) Pressure or constriction in chest. ___ Choking feelings...... ___ Sighings.............. ___ Dyspnea............... ___	____	

SCORING FOR HAMILTON ANXIETY:

0---------------1---------------2---------------3---------------4
None Mild Moderate Severe Very severe

HAMILTON ANXIETY	SEVERITY	HAMILTON DEPRESSION (circle item which applies)
11. Gastro-intestinal Symptoms: (1 m) Difficulty in swallowing, lump in throat................ ___ Wind.................. ___ Dyspepsia (nausea, vomiting, sour stomach).............. ___ "Working" in abdomen.. ___ Looseness of bowels... ___ Loss of weight........ ___ Constipation.......... ___	____	12. Somatic Symptoms Gastro-intestinal: 1 None 2 Loss of appetite but eating without staff encouragement; Heavy feeling in abdomen 3 Difficulty eating without staff urging. Requests or requires laxatives or medication for GI symptoms 16. Loss of Weight A. WHEN RATING BY HISTORY: 1 No weight loss 2 Probable weight loss associated with present illness 3 Definite (according to patient) weight loss B. WHEN ACTUAL WEIGHT CHANGES ARE MEASURED: 1 Less than 1 lb. loss in week 2 More than 1 lb. loss in week 3 More than 2 lbs. loss in week Rate A or B not both
12. Genito-urinary Symptoms: (1 m) Frequency of urination............. ___ Urgency of urination.. ___ Sexual dysfunction.... ___	____	14. Genital Symptoms: **Does your mood affect your sexual appetite or performance?** Symptoms such as: Loss of libido; Menstrual disturbance 1 Absent 2 Mild 3 Severe

SCORING FOR HAMILTON ANXIETY:

0---------------1---------------2---------------3---------------4
None Mild Moderate Severe Very severe

HAMILTON ANXIETY	SEVERITY	HAMILTON DEPRESSION (circle item which applies)
13. Autonomic Symptoms: (1 m) Dry mouth............. ___ Blushing/pallor....... ___ Tendency to sweat; clammy hands.......... ___ Dizziness, lightheadedness....... ___ Tension headache...... ___ Raising of hair....... ___	____	11. Anxiety Somatic: 1 Absent 2 Mild 3 Moderate 4 Severe 5 Incapacitating Physiological concomitants of anxiety, such as: Sweating, sighing; Gastro-intestinal: dry mouth, wind, indigestion, diarrhea, cramps, belching. Cardio-vascular: palpitations, headaches. Respiratory-hyperventilation. Urinary frequency.
14. Behavior at Interview (general): Tense, not relaxed, fidgeting; clenching hands, picking fingers, tics, restlessness, pacing, tremor of hands, furrowed brow, strained face, increased muscular tone, sighing respirations, facial pallor Behavioral (physiological): Swallowing, belching, high resting pulse rate, tremor, respiration rate over 20/min. Combine general and physiological for one rating	____	

SCORING FOR HAMILTON ANXIETY:

0---------------1---------------2---------------3---------------4
None Mild Moderate Severe Very severe

HAMILTON ANXIETY	SEVERITY	HAMILTON DEPRESSION (circle item which applies)
6. Depressed Mood: **Do you sometimes get down, blue, sad, depressed? How does this feeling affect your outlook on yourself, and the future?** 1 m Loss of interest...... ___ Lack of pleasure in hobbies............... ___ Depression............ ___ Early waking.......... ___ Diurnal swing......... ___ SCORE THIS ITEM AFTER SCORING HAMILTON DEPRESSION ITEMS: 1, 2, 7, 18, 22, 23, 24, 3.		1. Depressed Mood: Sadness, hopeless, helpless, worthless 1 Absent 2 These feeling states indicated only on questioning 3 These feeling states spontaneously reported verbally 4 Communicates feeling states non-verbally -- i.e., through facial expression, posture, voice and tendency to weep 5 Patient reports VIRTUALLY ONLY these feeling states in his spontaneous verbal and non-verbal communication

HAMILTON ANXIETY	HAMILTON DEPRESSION (Circle item which applies)
Item 6 cont'd	2. Feelings of Guilt: **Do you brood about past mistakes?** 1 Absent 2 Self-reproach, feels he/she has let people down 3 Ideas of guilt or rumination over past errors or sinful deeds 4 Present illness is a punishment. Delusions of guilt 5 Hears accusatory or denunciatory voices; experiences threatening visual hallucinations 7. Work and Activities: **Do you find it hard to get started doing things or have lost interest in things you normally enjoyed?** Do not include avoidance of activities due to phobic anxiety 1 No difficulty 2 Thoughts and feelings of incapacity, fatigue or weakness related to activities, work or hobbies 3 Loss of interest in hobbies or work - either directly in listlessness, indecision and vacillation (feels he has to push self to work/activities) 4 Decrease in actual time spent in productivity. In hospital, rate 4 if patient does not spend at least 3 hours a day in activities (hospital job or hobbies) 5 Stopped working because of present illness. In hospital, rate 5 if no activities except ward chores, or failure to do chores unassisted 18. Diurnal Variation: AM PM 1 1 Absent 2 2 Mild 3 3 Severe If depressive symptoms are worse in the AM or PM, note which it is and rate severity of variation
SCORE THIS ITEM AFTER SCORING HAMILTON DEPRESSION ITEMS: 1,2,7, 18,22,23,24,3	22. Helplessness: Is it hard for you to do simple or routine things for yourself? 1 Not present 2 Subjective feelings which are elicited only by inquiry 3 Patient volunteers his helpless feelings 4 REQUIRES urging, guidance and reassurance to accomplish ward chores or personal hygiene 5 Requires physical assistance for dress, grooming, eating, bedside tasks or personal hygiene

HAMILTON ANXIETY	HAMILTON DEPRESSION (circle item which applies)
Item 6 cont'd	23. <u>Hopelessness</u>: **Do you sometimes doubt that things will get better**? 1 Not present 2 Intermittently doubts that "things will improve" but can be reassured 3 Consistently feels "hopeless" but accepts reassurances 4 Expresses feelings of discouragement, despair, pessimism about future, which cannot be dispelled 5 Spontaneously and inappropriately perseverates, "I'll never get well" or its equivalent
	24. <u>Worthlessness</u>: **How do the problems you have affect your self esteem; how you feel about yourself**? Ranges from mild loss of esteem, feelings of inferiority, self-depreciation to delusional notions of worthlessness 1 Not present 2 Indicates feelings of worthlessness (loss of self-esteem) only on questioning 3 Spontaneously indicates feelings of worthlessness (loss of self-esteem) 4 Different from 3 by degree: Patient volunteers that he is "no good", "inferior", etc. 5 Delusional notions of worthlessness, i.e., "I am a heap of garbage" or its equivalent
SCORE ITEM 6 HERE ______	3. <u>Suicide</u>: **Have you ever felt that life isn't worth living or thought about killing yourself**? If YES, **What sorts of thoughts have these been**? 1 Absent 2 Feels life is not worth living 3 Wishes he were dead or any thoughts of possible death to self 4 Suicidal ideas or gesture 5 Attempts at suicide (any serious attempt rate 5)

HAMILTON ANXIETY	HAMILTON DEPRESSION (circle item which applies)
	15. Hypochondriasis: **Do you worry a lot about your health?** 1 Not present 2 Self-absorption (bodily) 3 Preoccupation with health 4 Frequent complaints, request for help, etc. 5 Hypochondriacal delusions
	17. Insight: 1 Acknowledges being depressed and ill 2 Acknowledges illness but attributes cause to bad food, climate, overwork, virus, need for rest, etc. 3 Denies being ill at all IF NOT DEPRESSED SCORE 1
	19. Depersonalization and Derealization: 1 Absent 2 Mild (Such as: Feeling of unreality-Nihilistic ideas) 3 Moderate 4 Severe 5 Incapacitating
	20. Paranoid Symptoms: 1 None 2 Suspicious 3 Ideas of reference 4 Delusions of reference and persecution 5 Hallucinations, persecutory
	21. Obsessional and Compulsive Symptoms: 1 Absent 2 Mild 3 Severe
	9. Agitation: 1 None 2 "Playing with" hands, hair, etc. 3 Hand-wringing, nail biting, hair-pulling, biting of lips
HAMILTON ANXIETY TOTAL ______	Subtotal ______ Correction -24 HAMILTON DEPRESSION TOTAL ______

SUMMARY

What is the primary problem you want help with?; What is the major change you would like to make?

Is there anything else that we haven't covered or that we haven't addressed sufficiently?

MENTAL STATUS

INTERVIEW BEHAVIOR

NOTES

NARRATIVE SUMMARY

This should include presenting complaint, history, diagnostic impression, etc.

CLINICIAN'S RATINGS AND DIAGNOSES

ABSENT		MILD		MODERATE		SEVERE		VERY SEVERE
0	1	2	3	4	5	6	7	8
None		Slightly disturbing/ not really disabling		Definitely disturbing/ disabling		Markedly disturbing/ disabling		Very severely disturbing/ disabling

CURRENT DSM-IV DIAGNOSES

	PRINCIPAL DIAGNOSIS	SEVERITY RATING	ADDITIONAL DIAGNOSES	SEVERITY RATING
AXIS I:	______	______	______	______
	______	______	______	______
			______	______
			______	______
			______	______
AXIS II:	______	______	______	______

AXIS III: ______________________

AXIS IV: Acute: __________ Enduring: __________

Stressors: ______________________

____

AXIS V: Present: __________ Last Year: __________

PAST DSM-IV DIAGNOSES

DIAGNOSIS	SEVERITY RATING	DATE OF ONSET	DATE OF REMISSION
______	______	______	______
______	______	______	______
______	______	______	______
______	______	______	______

Hamilton Anxiety: ______________ Hamilton Depression: ______________

Time: Start ______________ Stop ______________

Diagnostic confidence rating (0-100): __________ If rating is $\leq$ 70, please comment:

____

____

ADIS-IV Diagnostic Timeline (DTL)

Patient Name: ____________

Rater: ____ IV: ____________ ____________ ____________ ____________ ____________

LES-Ps:

LES-Os:

DOB ____________ DATE ____________

DIAG:

DOS:					
CONF #1:					
CONF #2:					

DOR:					
CONF #1:					
CONF #2:					

Confidence: 0 = not at all confident; 100 = definitely

Rater:	OS:					
Rater:	OR:					